Natives Are Restless
the

the Natives Are Restless

A SAN FRANCISCO DANCE MASTER TAKES HULA INTO THE 21ST CENTURY

Kumu Hula Patrick Makuakāne and Nā Lei Hulu i ka Wēkiu

CONSTANCE HALE

SparkPress with
Nā Lei Hulu i ka Wēkiu
San Francisco, California

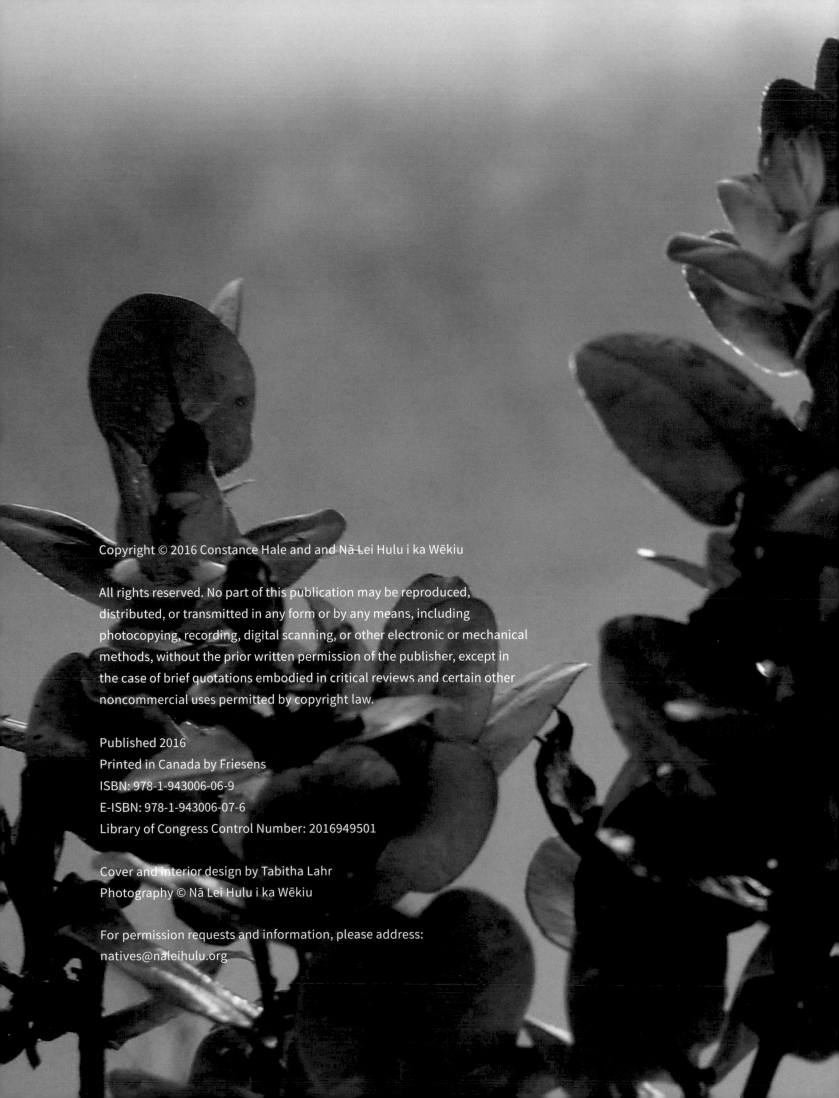

Published 2016
Printed in Canada by Friesens
ISBN: 978-1-943006-06-9
E-ISBN: 978-1-943006-07-6
Library of Congress Control Number: 2016949501

Cover and interior design by Tabitha Lahr
Photography © Nā Lei Hulu i ka Wēkiu

For permission requests and information, please address:
natives@naleihulu.org

For all our kumu

'A 'ohe hana nui ke alu 'ia
("No work is too great when done together by all")

Contents

"Onaona i ka Hala"

Preface

I am not the kind of person who talks to dead people. I don't testify. I leave spirits alone. And I tend to be skeptical of those who speak in tongues.

Yet every Wednesday evening, I throw on a T-shirt and a gathered cotton skirt, rush to an elementary school cafeteria in San Francisco, and proceed to whirl my arms, stamp my feet, and call out to figures like Pele (the goddess of the volcano), *ke akua i ka nāhelehele* (the god hidden in the mists of the low-hanging blood-red rainbow), and King Kalākaua (the Merrie Monarch of the nineteenth century). I do this in a guttural voice that would horrify a charm-school teacher and in a language that almost perished a hundred years ago.

Around me are dozens of other urbanites doing the same thing—my hula "brothers and sisters." Some are native Hawaiian; some are Samoan. Some are Korean, Filipino, Japanese, and Chinese. Some are Mexican, some Caucasian. Many are a mix of two or more of these. They may be eighteen years old or they may be eighty, but most are ordinary mortals like me: fiftysomething, more lumpy than lithe, and definitely not fitting the stereotype of what a hula dancer is supposed to look like.

"Ramkali"

"Noho Paipai"

We are the junior class of San Francisco's largest hula school, which also happens to be one of the largest hula schools in the world.

Many of us have been dancing here for years. We started by learning the basic steps of the ancient art form, which include the graceful *kāholo,* the movement most people associate with hula. That's when we move side to side, letting our hips flow in patterns as smooth as shore waves. We added the awkward-at-first *'uehe*—those hips keep moving while our knees take us into a plié and then suddenly pop out to each side, shaping our legs into hollow diamonds. Then we tackled eight other odd-seeming steps.

Eventually, we graduated to a few classic dances, two honoring Kalākaua and a third reminiscing about a composer's childhood home on Maui.

Soon, we progressed to sassy numbers heralding everything from the dainty "cheeks" of a beloved to the suggestive swaying of a boat. There's often more to the lyrics than the innocuous titles imply. In "Noho Paipai," for example, the rocking chair of the title is hardly a soothing instrument of maternal love; instead, the coy dancer invites a watching *malihini* (newcomer) to touch noses and share a breath—a traditional Hawaiian greeting—then join a wild ride on the "rocking chair." We learn that we must master athletic moves and signal to our audience the meanings hidden in the metaphors—through a mischievous smile, an especially deep hip undulation, or a provocative wink.

Whatever their tone and range, all of these dances have the same profound relationship to Hawaiian culture and history.

"Hula is the language of the heart and therefore the heartbeat of the Hawaiian people," Kalākaua said in the mid-1800s. For centuries before him, hula was the history book, children's literature, and sacred text of

Kumu Hula Patrick Makuakāne (far left) and Nā Lei Hulu i ka Wēkiu

a people with no written language. It maintained the relationship between gods and mortals. It preserved the greatness of the chiefly lines. It honored the race and encouraged procreation, and it traced the subtleties of the natural world: the rolling of waves onshore; the tumbling of waterfalls; the distinctions between tropical mists, showers, and rains.

But Kalākaua couldn't have guessed that hula's domain would widen so dramatically. Not only would it become essential in preserving a culture battered by European and American influences, it would also claim pride of place in the twenty-first century alongside hip-hop, Cajun, tango, and other popular forms of dance. Nor could Kalākaua have known that one hula master would reinvent the dance form in a way that would retain some of the most sacred and sensual moves his teachers taught him, but also throw in a little Hollywood, a bit of Broadway, or a subversive dose of the San Francisco club scene. In doing so, he would not just rock the stages of San Francisco, New York, New Orleans, and Honolulu but also prod, disturb, reinforce, and upend notions of what hula is, has been, and ever will be.

That master is my own teacher, Kumu Hula Patrick Makuakāne. Through him and his hula troupe, Nā Lei Hulu i ka Wēkiu, this book tells the largely untold story of a hula culture that has survived—and thrived—after more than a century of overt suppression and benign neglect. According to the Web site Mele.com, more than five hundred hula schools are spreading the dance form across the United States—not just in San Francisco, but in Portland, Pittsburgh, Chicago, and Charlotte. There are also schools in El Paso, Texas, and, of course, Aloha, Oregon.

Hula has also taken root in other countries and continents, with schools in Paris, Salzburg, and Singapore. Among the hundreds of schools in Japan is Hulabootie in Tokyo. Out of thirty-five schools in Mexico City alone, there is Estudio de Danza Polonesia Hine Ahu One.

But this story can be understood only in the larger context of Hawaiian history, which hula explores and celebrates. So I will also trace the key steps in that timeline, including the backstory of the archipelago in the early eighteenth century, with its rich indigenous culture; the arrival of Europeans in the later part of that century; the nineteenth-century betrayal of the people by American missionaries and mercantilists; the ravages of Western diseases; the loss of Hawaiians' independent kingdom in 1893; and the century of decline that followed, when the indigenous language, music, and dance all almost vanished.

The story culminates, of course, in the present, with Kumu Patrick, as I shall call him, and his *hālau,* or traditional school of hula, which is now thirty years old. Two decades ago, Kumu Patrick was a controversial choreographer. Since then, he has became a fixture in the San Francisco ethnic-dance world and a respected teacher in Hawai'i. To audiences, he is the friendly MC with the fearful biceps, the fierce chanter with the rich baritone, the eminently charming host in bare feet. Lordly in his presence, conversational in his patter, passionate about his craft, never afraid to pick up the *'ukulele* and strum, he inhabits a role he has created for himself: demystifier-in-chief of Hawaiian culture, but one who is pushing the envelope, too. His productions have evolved into multimedia spectaculars featuring all manner of music. Behind the dancers float projected illustrations of everyone from Pele to King Kalākaua to Louis Armstrong. (Who knew that Satchmo did a *Jazz Goes Hawaiian* album?)

There's a Hawaiian term, hard to translate, that helps explain the nature of Kumu Patrick's mission. The word is *kuleana,* and it can mean "inherited property," "privilege," "right," and "responsibility." It can also mean "concern" and "a calling." Kumu Patrick believes his kuleana is to preserve the tradition that has been given to him, but also to extend it for his own, very postmodern, purposes. That has made some people excited and others upset, as you would expect anytime a tradition gets remade. But his invention of a new dance style, *hula mua,* grows out of a determination to let Hawaiian culture be a living, breathing thing—something sacred that is never a sacred cow.

I have my own kuleana in telling Kumu Patrick's story. I started dancing the hula at age seven, on the North Shore of O'ahu. I also danced ballet from the ages of four through fourteen, then switched to jazz in high school, modern in college, and salsa as a young adult. For a few years, I abandoned dance, but not my love of the arts, nor my fascination with Hawaiian culture. At the Graduate School of Journalism at UC Berkeley, I wrote my master's thesis on Hawaiian slack-key guitar.

I went on to have a career as a reporter and editor, and I wrote about Hawai'i whenever I could: profiles of Hawaiian musicians, features on the sovereignty movement, travel essays about island cowboys, and "brights" about 'Iolani Palace and that island delicacy Spam musubi.

In 1997, I returned to dancing the hula by enrolling in a class with Kumu Patrick, who had been a source in an article I wrote for the *San Francisco Chronicle.* He continued to be helpful to me as I wrote about the hula for *Honolulu* magazine and the *Atlantic.* More important, we have collaborated for the past fifteen years on the annual newsletter for his hālau, *Kaholo'ana.*

Always, I have tried to write with a journalist's requisite detachment, but my crazy hula-love frames the work. My own kuleana is to share the knowledge that has been given to me about the tragic history of a fierce, exuberant, and resilient people—and to tell the deep, sexy, funny, multicultural story of hula through the lens of one of its most innovative practitioners.

"Aia i Waimānalo Kō Nuʻa Hulu"

"Salva Mea"

Introduction

The words of Rev. Hiram Bingham reverberate in a godlike, bass voice through a darkened San Francisco theater: *"The appearance of destitution, degradation, and barbarism among the chattering and almost naked savages was appalling."*

Scarlet and indigo lights begin to illuminate two dozen women seated on the stage, hunched over at the waist. Their costumes—voluminous skirts of crimson and gold; spiky headdresses—suggest the primitive culture Bingham deplores.

"This was a dark and ruined land whose people were filled with unrighteousness, fornication, wickedness, murder, debate, deceit, malignancy—whisperers, backbiters, haters of God . . . without natural affection."

The dancers begin to stir, and the words of another missionary linger in the air: *"I declare that the hula is a devil's nest, in which he looks about, rears himself up, and sniffs for the person he wishes to swallow."*

In the half-light, as the women sit upright, we realize that they are topless, their torsos bearing nothing but bold black tattoos.

The lights go down and the women exit. Next, tattooed men creep across the stage to the electronic track "Reverence." A shirtless, muscular chanter seated behind them begins to intone in Hawaiian (*"Kāua i ka makani o Nu'uanu . . ."*), accompanied by the powerful rhythms of an *ipu heke,* or double-gourd drum. The men respond, their fierce dance accented by the slapping of palms, the stamping of feet, and the clacking of anklets. The breathtaking tableau makes a mockery of Bingham's words. The dancers are sublime in their natural beauty and strength.

The music shifts again, and the women return, this time more covered. They move across the stage in oddly balletic movements, crossing, crisscrossing, forming, reforming.

In the final scene, the rest of the dancers return as Christian hymns are overlaid with contemporary "house" music. The dancers congregate on a stage that's been converted into an outdoor parish. The women wear long black skirts and high-collared blouses, the men black slacks and white button-down shirts. A syncretic montage now erupts, volcanically, with the relentless beat: images of reverence (hands clasped in prayer), of torment (a priest ripping at a convert's hair), of grace (kneeling dancers singing an ode to Jesus), and of melancholy (the women's long arms arcing downward, softly, gracefully, heartbreakingly).

Bingham would still be scandalized.

Chances are, when you hear the word *hula,* such emotional intensity does not come to mind. Perhaps you conjure an image of lovely girls in cellophane skirts, swaying their hips and waving their arms while Bing Crosby sings "Sweet Leilani." You might even think of Hula-Hoops—the plastic playthings invented in the 1950s and confused, to this day, with the ancient art form. But, for sure, you do not imagine a dark-skinned priest with a severe face and a long black vestment, committing violence against women in Victorian costumes.

Welcome to the world of Kumu Hula Patrick Makuakāne and his San Francisco hula troupe, Nā Lei Hulu i ka Wēkiu.

Kumu Patrick has been choreographing daring shows like this one for three decades, using them to explore some of the most turbulent aspects of Hawaiian history. But that's not all he does with hula.

Some of his pieces simply strip the dance of its touristy clichés and present it in its purest form. They might be examples of hula in the ancient style, danced to the fierce beat of a sharkskin drum, praising long-gone chiefs. Or they might be delicate dances complemented by guitars and 'ukulele, affirming the value of enduring love through poetic metaphors and lyrical movements.

Then there are the full-length repertory works. Some, like *The Natives Are Restless* (which inspired the title of this book), explore the history of an indigenous people and the fatal intrusion of the West. Some tell ancient stories—like the 2008 show *Māui: Turning Back the Sky*—and generate signature numbers like "He Wahine Namunamu," where women performers beat imaginary bark cloth on wooden anvils, as did their ancient ancestors, pleading with the Polynesian hero Māui to slow down the sun. Still others feature an anthology of traditional standards like "Pua 'Āhihi," a melodious twentieth-century love song about a particular blossom and the mysterious peak Lanihuli, on the windward side of O'ahu, where that flower finds shelter.

Included in this repertoire are the pieces in which Kumu Patrick radically upends tradition and brings hula raging into the twenty-first century. He has invented a new style that he calls "progressive hula": he sets traditional movements to tunes by Annie Lennox, say, or opera by Léo Delibes, or soundscapes by Dead Can

"He Wahine Namunamu"

"Lakme"

Dance. These hula numbers appear within his larger works, or by themselves, or in extravaganzas like the one in New Orleans on Halloween in 1997, when the group seized an ice-skating rink, converted it into a dance club, and, in front of eight thousand costumed revelers, danced to "Odyssey to Anyoona" by the German trance duo Jam & Spoon.

His genre-bending numbers are accompanied by lighting and visual effects that create a similar mash-up. The collision of images makes for a mad mix of tradition and "street." It creates a kind of synesthesia in the audience, a response to the various musical, movement, and multimedia experiences.

This hula is primal, archetypal, comic, esoteric, big of heart, and bound to surprise. It works like poetry, causing the imagination to fire in unexpected ways.

"Makuakāne is a master teacher, a star performer, and also a community organizer of formidable talents," writes dance critic Paul Parish. "He looks like Michelangelo's Adam in a grass skirt, dances like a god,

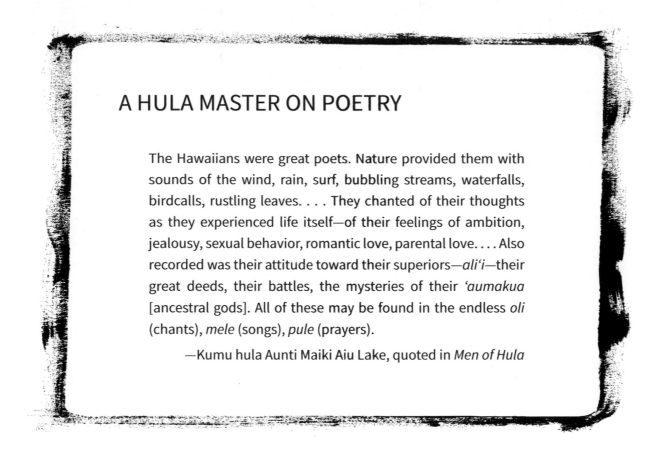

A HULA MASTER ON POETRY

The Hawaiians were great poets. **Nature** provided them with sounds of the wind, rain, surf, **bubbling** streams, waterfalls, birdcalls, rustling leaves. . . . **They chanted of their thoughts** as they experienced life itself—of their feelings of ambition, jealousy, sexual behavior, romantic love, parental love. . . . Also recorded was their attitude **toward their superiors**—*ali'i*—their great deeds, their battles, the mysteries of their *'aumakua* [ancestral gods]. All of these may be found in the endless *oli* (chants), *mele* (songs), *pule* (prayers).

—Kumu hula Aunti Maiki Aiu Lake, quoted in *Men of Hula*

sings like a cantor, and works the crowd like Bill Clinton. . . . He's not only keeping Hawaiian culture alive, he's a populist making the case for it. Though he's serious, he is in no way grindingly earnest. In fact, his sense of humor can get riotous."

Think Alvin Ailey rewired, Mark Morris run amok on a Pacific island.

The story of Kumu Patrick Makuakāne and his school of hula cannot be told in a vacuum. For it is also the story of Hawai'i, whose original settlers are believed to have arrived in two waves during the great era of Polynesian voyages exploring the Pacific, which ended around 1300—from the Marquesas Islands as early as the third century AD and from the Society Islands (including Tahiti) as early as the eighth and as late as the fourteenth century.

The legends and mythology these islanders brought with them were as complex and heroic as those of the ancient Greeks and Romans. "The ancient Hawaiians were very aware of the special beauties of their place in the world," writes Rita Ariyoshi in *Hula Is Life*. "Their legends and poetry, expressed in the chants and hula, would, if they were more widely known, take their place beside the Homeric voyages, the adventures of Cuchulainn, the Ramayana epic, Norse sagas, and Icelandic myths. Without a written language, it was hula that kept the history of the Hawaiian people. It told their stories; it still does."

The landing of British Captain James Cook in 1778 and the subsequent arrival of European and American whalers, missionaries, and merchants did not bode well for the vulnerable Hawaiian archipelago of eight major islands. In the following two centuries, the Hawaiian population was decimated by disease, its kingdom overthrown, and its surviving people dispersed through diaspora.

"'O ka Au Moana"

"Kaulīlua i ke Anu Wai'ale'ale"

The hula suffered through this story of loss. Bob Krauss, in the *Honolulu Advertiser,* called hula at once the best known and the least understood of the fine arts in Hawai'i. "First," he wrote, "the missionaries condemned it to hell fire. Then Tin Pan Alley turned it into a dance no self-respecting Hawaiian would perform." After Hawai'i became a state in 1959, tourism and urbanization proved as devastating to hula as had the missionaries and the movies. As the skyrocketing cost of living drove many Native Hawaiians to the mainland, hula, along with the rest of Hawaiian culture, was in danger of extinction.

But it survived, and eventually a resurrection began to take hold. A cultural reawakening swept the islands, inspired by the activism on the mainland in the '60s and fueled by a potent mix of antidevelopment anger and ethnic pride. Interest in crafts like featherwork and musical composition surged. Traditional navigational practices were reinvigorated, and pride in Polynesian know-how swelled as the double-hulled canoe *Hōkūle'a* sailed to Tahiti in 1976. Elderly masters of *lua* (martial arts) were tracked down and the training of warriors reborn. Students filled Hawaiian-language preschools and bilingual-immersion elementary schools. Hawaiian Language became the hot course at the University of Hawai'i.

Young people flooded into hula schools. Professional dancers who had mastered the hulas of the tourism industry sought out older practitioners and cultural experts and passed on their traditional practices. The Merrie

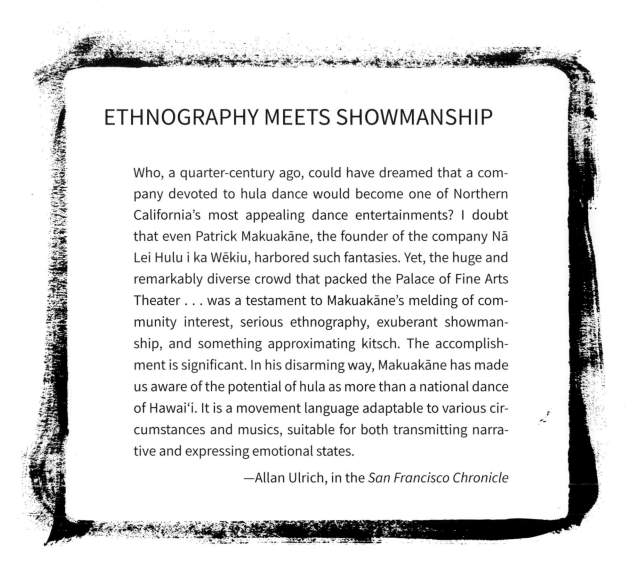

ETHNOGRAPHY MEETS SHOWMANSHIP

Who, a quarter-century ago, could have dreamed that a company devoted to hula dance would become one of Northern California's most appealing dance entertainments? I doubt that even Patrick Makuakāne, the founder of the company Nā Lei Hulu i ka Wēkiu, harbored such fantasies. Yet, the huge and remarkably diverse crowd that packed the Palace of Fine Arts Theater . . . was a testament to Makuakāne's melding of community interest, serious ethnography, exuberant showmanship, and something approximating kitsch. The accomplishment is significant. In his disarming way, Makuakāne has made us aware of the potential of hula as more than a national dance of Hawai'i. It is a movement language adaptable to various circumstances and musics, suitable for both transmitting narrative and expressing emotional states.

—Allan Ulrich, in the *San Francisco Chronicle*

Monarch Festival in Hilo started promoting the art of hula in 1964, and it soon grew into an annual blockbuster event. The Kamehameha Schools in Honolulu brought Hawaiian studies, which they called "Hawaiiana," which included hula, into the curriculum. And visionary *kumu hula,* or masters of dance, started setting up traditional dance schools, or *hālau hula,* as they were rechristened.

The movement gained force and later became known as the Hawaiian Cultural Renaissance. Scholars, teachers, and practitioners took on the formidable task of bringing Hawaiian culture back from the brink, clinching hula's reemergence.

One of those figures was Aunti Maiki Aiu Lake, a kumu hula who transformed the teaching of the dance. Kumu Patrick studied under two of her protégés while he was in high school (and under a third more recently). From these teachers, he gained a foundation in the esoteric traditions of hula. But he was part of a group of native Hawaiian artists—kumu hula; musicians; composers; and long-distance, open-ocean wayfinders—who have distinguished themselves from earlier practitioners. For the previous generation, the question central to their work was *whether* Hawaiian culture would survive. But because Kumu Patrick and his peers came of age creatively after the Hawaiian Cultural Renaissance, they were free to focus more on *how* it will survive. They have shown that their own mission is not so much to revive the culture as to deliver it, kicking, into the twenty-first century.

"I'm part of the older cohort," says Puakea Nogelmeier, a professor of Hawaiian language at the University of Hawai'i–Mānoa and also a kumu hula. His colleagues, he explains, are the preservationists who saw a culture waning and mobilized to conserve what was almost lost. But the next generation was different, he says. "They don't have that intense burden of saving the culture; they are exploring, and moving from preservation to innovation."

Not all innovation is welcomed by every authority in the hula world. The author and ethnomusicologist Amy Kuʻuleialoha Stillman points out that today, "forces are operating in multiple directions—it's not a black-and-white thing." She emphasizes that hula's spread across the mainland and the globe presents new challenges to the innovators. "There's a delicate balance between what a kumu is able to share and the ʻano, or consciousness, of the students," she says. "You don't want to produce automatons, but you also don't want to just capitalize on universalist notions of spirituality wrapped in mysticism. What are we allowing in the name of Hawaiian culture?"

This is the context in which Kumu Patrick is working as both cultural practitioner and ambitious choreographer. His innovations form the heart of this book, which attempts to balance the story of this ethnic dance tradition with the story of its contemporary edge. From the ancient Hawaiian chant *The Kumulipo* come dances in which nature is foregrounded and sexuality celebrated. From the San Francisco club underground comes the inspiration for "Salva Mea," in which Christianity battles for supremacy with Hawaiian polyamory. From the nineteenth century's poetry and the twentieth century's Madonna come the inspiration for "Rain," in which women in blue velvet dresses sway to music by the bad girl of pop. From a deeply felt love of place—the source of so many nostalgic *mele ʻāina,* or "songs of the land"—comes the inspiration for "I Left My Heart in San Francisco." From flash mobs come the inspiration for *Hit & Run Hula,* in which scores of dancers jump out of city buses, Hawaiian Airlines seats, and crowds in Times Square to dance the "He Inoa No Auntie Genoa Keawe Pāpālina Disco Mega Mix."

Lest you think that Kumu Patrick has scorned tradition, we will also look at how fervently he is perpetuating the rites and rituals of hula. He begins every class with *hula kahiko,* the style of dance prevalent before Europeans came to Hawaiʻi. These dances—primal, percussive, sexual, and powerful—praise the gods, honor the chiefs, and express all kinds of love. They are followed, in class, by *hula ʻauana,* the graceful, sensuous, and playful dances that celebrate beautiful flowers, handsome ships, or famous firemen. We will watch his students master "Pua Līlīlehua," a love song written for his teacher's teacher. Its unhurried vamps and fluid gestures do his hula grandmother proud.

"I am not trying to turn hula on its head," Kumu Patrick says. "I appreciate our traditions. In fact, I insist that all my students are grounded in traditional dance and in Hawaiian values: discipline, integrity, attentiveness, respect, a sense of family, and a sense of *aloha,* or loving-kindness.

"But we don't live in a vacuum," he adds. "I want hula to express every aspect of my life as a contemporary Hawaiian. I want to push the boundaries with choreography and chanting and music, but also with lighting, sound, graphics, and multimedia. Hula should be as layered as my life and as dynamic as any other dance form."

"I Left My Heart in San Francisco," honoring Tony Bennett (seated)

OUR
HULA LINEAGE

Keahi Luahine, 'Ilālā'ole,
Kapua (Keahi's cousin)

Kawena Pukui
Keaka Kanahele (for *hula pahu*)

Lōkālia Montgomery

Aunti Maiki (Maiki Aiu Lake)

John Keola
Lake

Robert Uluwehi
Cazimero

Mae Kamāmalu
Klein

Patrick Makuakāne

PART I

Moʻokūʻauhau ("Origins")

Moʻokūʻauhau can be translated as "genealogy," as well as "origins." Embedded in it is the word *kūʻauhau,* which might be translated as "pedigree," "lineage," or "old traditions." But *kūʻauhau* also refers to a particular class of genealogical prayer chant. The name contains a clue to the Hawaiian way of thinking about origins. As scholar Martha Warren Beckwith suggests, the idea of genealogy in Hawaiʻi might be less like a tree, with myriad branches and leaves, and more like the many meanderings of a roadway that is trod on by human feet and contains junctures and crisscrossing forces.

"Hānau ka ʻUku Koʻakoʻa"

CHAPTER ONE

The Kumulipo
(The Beginning in Deep Darkness)

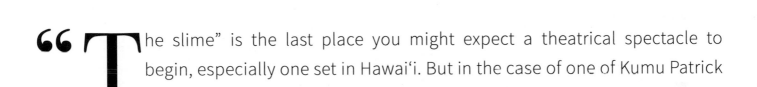

"The slime" is the last place you might expect a theatrical spectacle to begin, especially one set in Hawai'i. But in the case of one of Kumu Patrick Makuakāne's signature works, slime it is.

Or, to be more exact, "the deep darkness" referred to by the word *kumulipo*—the time before humanity, before animals, before land, before sand.

In the suite of dances called *The Kumulipo,* this is also the deep darkness of the theater when all the lights are turned off, when the heavy velvet curtain is drawn, when the music hasn't begun.

Then it does begin—a bass beat, heavier than a heartbeat. Three electronic pulses, then a pause; three electronic pulses, then a pause.

The curtain opens. We are in the Palace of Fine Arts Theatre, yes, but we are also underwater, listening to that beat and looking up at a huge image of the underwater world projected at the back of the stage. At the surface, the sea roils, shades of gray and turquoise. Somewhere, far away, floats a large orb: the sun. Rays of golden light slice through our undersea world.

"Hānau ke Poʻo Waʻawaʻa"

The water undulates, and an electronic hum joins the throbbing beat. The music undulates, too, changing key, stretching, moving. Then a voice. A human voice, a baritone note over the bass beat. Words form, amplified through the theater, intoning centuries-old Hawaiian lines: *O ke au i kahuli wela ka honua* . . .

Forms emerge in the onstage darkness. Dim forms, round forms, indistinguishable in the dark and in the mist that swirls around them.

In an urgent, plaintive voice, the chanter continues. Behind the chanting, underneath the chanting, around the chanting, the electronic hum swells, and different instruments call out and then disappear, passing through the dark theater—drifting, diminishing. The forms are ambiguous, the music fluid but undefined. This is the soundscape of scary movies, of dark dreams, of the primordial swamp.

Then, suddenly, the last words are belted out: *Hānau ka pō!* The night is born!

A moment of silence. Then a familiar boom—the sharp slap of a bare hand on a double-gourd drum. The beat takes off—rhythmic, familiar. An eerie, neon blue light suffuses the stage. The formless shapes onstage rustle, stretch, stand. They begin to extend limbs and then quickly retract them, repeating these fierce, angular movements over and over. They are men and women, dressed in layered cloth skirts, their wrists and ankles circled with *kukui* nuts, their heads crowned with spiky ferns and delicate moss.

In the half-light, the chanter is revealed: Kumu Patrick Makuakāne, his chest bare, his muscled arms encircling his gourd drum. Behind all of the human figures, on the large screen, the shifting sea fades out and the long, tubular tendrils of coral polyps fade in, arching over the dancers' heads.

The world is beginning to take shape. And it's in Technicolor.

SACRED SPARKS

We in the audience slowly focus on one more element in addition to lights, photo montage, costumes, and choreography: Projected on dark screens at each side of the stage is text that scrolls from floor to ceiling. Crisp white words rise eloquent on lava black.

The text on the left unfolds in Hawaiian:

O ke au i kahuli wela ka honua
O ke au i kahuli lole ka lani
O ke au i kukaʻiaka ka lā.

The text on the right unfolds in English:

Heated by the sun
it was time for the earth
to produce
Exposed to view
time for the sky
to impregnate
Its essence overshadowing
time for the sun to caress.

"Hānau ka I'a"

These are the first lines of *The Kumulipo,* a 2,102-line chant that describes, in poetic imagery, the first spark of life in the universe and the evolution of all life forms as ancient Hawaiians understood them—from coral polyps to contemporary people, from flora to fauna, from primary gods to mythological heroes, from Father Sky and Mother Earth to very specific genealogical pairs that carried a sacred line of chiefs to the flesh-and-blood world of eighteenth-century Hawai'i.

The more precise name of the chant is *kumu-(u)-li-po,* "beginning (in) the deep darkness." The word is composed of two key parts: *kumu* means "source" or "beginnings," and *lipo* "deep darkness"—the dark of the depth of a cavern, or the darkness of the depth of the sea. *Kumu* is also used for "teacher," the source of knowledge and tradition. *Lipo* is used to describe the ocean bottom, where lies the *walewale,* or slime, out of which all life emerges.

The chant is indeed about all life emerging, expressing truly Polynesian concepts of origin, so it is often referred to as a Hawaiian creation myth. The more accurate term might be "genealogical prayer chant," for it traces *one family's* divine origin—from its inception at the dawn of time, through mythological ancestors, through a line of literal ancestors of current rulers. And in ancient times, many such chants might have existed. Each major chiefly line would have possessed its own genealogy chant—the poetry being as sacred to the family as a crown or a sword or a scepter might be to Western royals.

Traditionally, chants like *The Kumulipo* would be kept by the family whose evolution they describe. A chant would enhance the prestige of the family, since it traced the family back to the beginning of time,

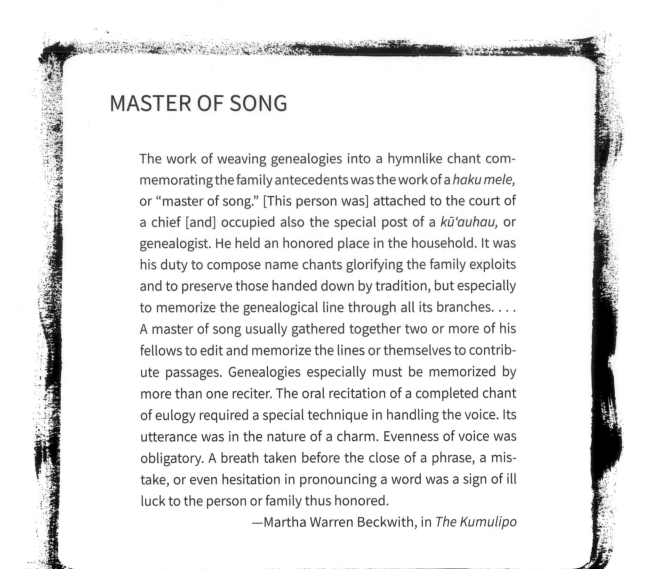

MASTER OF SONG

The work of weaving genealogies into a hymnlike chant commemorating the family antecedents was the work of a *haku mele,* or "master of song." [This person was] attached to the court of a chief [and] occupied also the special post of a *kūʻauhau,* or genealogist. He held an honored place in the household. It was his duty to compose name chants glorifying the family exploits and to preserve those handed down by tradition, but especially to memorize the genealogical line through all its branches. . . . A master of song usually gathered together two or more of his fellows to edit and memorize the lines or themselves to contribute passages. Genealogies especially must be memorized by more than one reciter. The oral recitation of a completed chant of eulogy required a special technique in handling the voice. Its utterance was in the nature of a charm. Evenness of voice was obligatory. A breath taken before the close of a phrase, a mistake, or even hesitation in pronouncing a word was a sign of ill luck to the person or family thus honored.

—Martha Warren Beckwith, in *The Kumulipo*

but it would remain shrouded in secrecy because of its magical, religious, and political value. In its entirety, it would be memorized only by successive teams of chanters—always at least two, so that the information would not be lost.

Scholars consider *The Kumulipo* the most authentic of such chants in Hawaiian literature. It was inherited by King Kalākaua, having been composed for his great-great-great-grandfather Ka-ʻi-ʻi-Mamao. It linked the newborn and his offspring to all things great and small—on the earth, in the sea, in the heavens, in the spirit world, and in the world of living people.

Kalākaua published *The Kumulipo* in Hawaiian in 1889 as part of a campaign to establish his legitimate right to the throne. Foreign power had been increasing in the islands, and class distinctions were falling away, but the kingdom's subjects still placed paramount importance on hereditary rank. Kalākaua seized on the chance to preserve his family's claim to great prestige.

In 1897, his sister, Queen Liliʻuokalani, published the poem's first English translation, which she had begun, line by line, when she was held prisoner at Washington Place after being deposed—and while watching revolutionary forces work to bring her once-sovereign nation under the control of the United States.

THE POETRY

The Kumulipo has since been translated by various scholars and experts. They offer differing interpretations of its allusions, symbols, metaphors, and sounds—which themselves create a tapestry of hidden meanings.

The most preeminent of those scholars, Martha Warren Beckwith, compares *The Kumulipo* to Greek creation chants—especially Hesiod's *Theogony*—as well as to the Hebrew *Genesis*. Beckwith says the Greek counterpart is more thematically similar in that there, too, the world is believed to have taken shape—or been born—as the natural product of parental mating, rather than directly through the will of God. But in "poetic splendor and artistic worth," she writes, *The Kumulipo* has more in common with *Genesis*.

The first half of the chant details the lively progression from primal slime to animal, plant, and human forms. It opens in the world of *pō* (night/darkness/the spirit world) and describes the species of plants and animals that are born (*hānau*) or come forth (*puka*).

The first verse sets the time (when the heat of the earth rose, when the winter was in its deepest night, when the slime covered the earth, when night was born). The next introduces the forms that start to emerge from the muck:

"Hānau ka ʻUku Koʻakoʻa"

Kumulipo was born in the night, a male.

Poele was born in the night, a female.

A coral insect was born, from which was born perforated coral.

The earthworm was born, which gathered earth into mounds.

From it were born worms full of holes.

The starfish was born, whose children were born starry.

The phosphorous was born, whose children were born phosphorescent.

The poet-composer of *The Kumulipo* hits upon a device similar to the one the Greeks used in their creation chants. As the litany progresses, one animal is born from another, or one plant from another, in a steady rhythmic progression. In some lines, a parent is paired with a child, as in this sequence describing the emergence of shellfish:

The Hāwaʻe (smooth sea urchin) was born,
 his child the Wana-ku (long-spiked sea urchin) came forth.
The Hāʻukeʻuke (ring-shaped sea urchin) was born,
 his child the Uhalula (thin-spiked sea urchin) came forth.
The Pīʻoe (barnacle) was born,
 his child the Pipi (pearl oyster) came forth.
The Pāpaua (mother-of-pearl) was born,
 his child the ʻŌlepe (oyster) came forth.
The Nahawele (mussel) was born,
 his child the Unauna (hermit crab) came forth.
The Makaiaulu (big limpet) was born,
 his child the ʻOpihi (small limpet) came forth.

In other lines, a water species (for example, *ʻekaha*, a sea moss) is paired with a land species (like *ʻekahakaha*, a land fern). Here we begin to see the intricacy of the poetry: the creatures of sea and forest are linked not only by color and shape, but also by their names themselves:

Born was the ʻĒkaha (moss) living in the sea
 guarded by the ʻĒkahakaha (fern) living in the forest…
Born was the Kōʻele (seaweed) living in the sea
 guarded by the Kō Punapuna Kōʻeleʻele (long-joined sugarcane) living in the forest…
Born was the Hulu-waena (hairy seaweed) living in the sea
 guarded by the Huluhulu Ieie (hairy pandanus vine) in the forest…

Next, the chant transitions to the time of *ao* (day/light/the world of living people). At this point in creation, gods and humans are introduced into the landscape. The lines of poetry are filled with sexual innuendos evoking the reproductive process—from "the woman who sits sideways" to the rubbing of the "female firestick" to produce sparks. (Then there is *keakea*, which might mean "very white" or "a towhead," unless it means "semen." Or unless it's spelled *keʻa*, which might be a crucifix, a dart, or a virile male.)

Repetition underscores the exuberant waxing of the race. "Born were people by the hundreds," the chant exclaims. "People stood together . . . People slept together . . . Wave after wave of people . . . Hundreds upon hundreds of chiefs."

The poem blends three myths about the parenthood of humankind. First is the myth of Laʻilaʻi, the mother of gods and humans. The name Laʻilaʻi means "calmness," but she is also described as "trembling" before the "hot, rumbling heaven." She joins with Kiʻi, a man, producing children with a "ruddy tint" and "fine, reddish hair at puberty." She joins with Kāne, a god, producing Kanaloa, the hot-striking octopus.

Then she produces multitudes—first, the women:

Born was Groping-one (Hahapoele), a girl.
Born was Dim-sighted (Ha-popo), a girl.
Born was Beautiful (Maila) called Clothed-in-leaves (Lopalapala)…

"Hānau ka Naonao"

In other lines come the myths of Haumea and the god Kanaloa (in which Haumea's children were "born from the brain") and the myth of Papa (Mother Earth) and Wākea (Father Sky). In the latter myth, the warm upper layer of earth hosts the fertilized seed, which awaits the rain from heaven and the warm sun to help it spring to life.

Meanwhile, the children keep tumbling out—the little ones, the older ones—including Creeping-ti-plant, Expected-day, and the twins Midnight and First-light. "Ever increasing in number," the chant continues, "humanity spread abroad." And, finally, "It was Day."

This orgiastic romp through earth, sky, volcanic hillsides, and sacred forests is reflected in the poetry—in alliteration and assonance, allusions and symbols. Then, suddenly, the chant settles down. In fact, starting with line 708, the final verses of *The Kumulipo* are far less fetching poetically, though important politically: in place of epic storytelling and poetic language, we get the more prosaic business of listing genealogical pairs—one male and one female—whose various branches make up the final family lines of descent. Those genealogical duos come straightforwardly, one after another: four hundred pairs of names.

THE DANCE

In 2009, when Kumu Patrick was anticipating the twenty-fifth anniversary of his hālau, he burned to choreograph something that would dig deep into Hawaiian tradition. So when he received a San Francisco Arts Commission grant to create a new work, he chose the iconic Hawaiian creation chant as his starting point for a suite of "dance narratives." *The Kumulipo: An Homage* opened the second act of Nā Lei Hulu's October 2010 show.

In keeping with his habit of breaking new ground, Kumu Patrick relied on a completely new translation of the ancient chant. That text was the result of thirty years of study by Lucia Tarallo Jensen, whose scholarly research has inspired other Nā Lei Hulu works, including *Daughters of Haumea* (chapter four) and *Māui: Turning Back the Sky.* "Lucia is a mentor who prods me to think more deeply about *kānaka maoli* life," Kumu Patrick notes, using the Hawaiian term for the people of Hawai'i. "She challenges me to dig into the esoteric trenches and relinquish Western preconceptions and ideals. I find it invigorating."

For her part, Jensen says that, in translating the text, she wanted to *create,* rather than *regurgitate.* She

WHAT'S IN A FEW WORDS?

The many scholars, translators, and historians who have interpreted *The Kumulipo* often disagree. To grasp the complexity of this task of translation, we don't have to look further than the first two lines:

O ke au i kahuli wela ka honua
O ke au i kahuli lole ka lani.

Queen Liliʻuokalani translated these lines as:

At the time that turned the heat of the earth
At the time when the heavens turned and changed.

A subsequent translator, Pokini Robinson, believed that the opening lines of the chant herald the birth not just of the natural universe but also of a child, whose stages of development are chronicled in succeeding sections of the chant. So she rendered the same lines differently:

The time of the birth of the taboo chief
The time when the heavenly one pushed his way out.

The contemporary scholar Lucia Tarallo Jensen translates the chant's opening lines this way:

Heated by the sun, it was time for Earth to produce!
Exposed to view, time for the sky to impregnate!

Various interpretations are laid out in Martha Warren Beckwith's landmark 1951 book, *The Kumulipo: A Hawaiian Creation Chant.* Another good source is by Rubellite Kawena Johnson: *Kumulipo: The Hawaiian Hymn of Creation, Volume 1, Chants 1 & 2,* published in 1981. Jensen's translation has not yet been published.

views *The Kumulipo* less as a genealogical document and more as an ode to nature—one that teaches us about the kuleana, or responsibility, of each human who shares in its bounty. We must all, she notes, ensure that all elements continue to exist in harmony.

In the movement from pō (the world of darkness, night, spirits) to ao (the world of light, day, humanity), she sees an expression of the essential duality of the Hawaiian worldview, in which every part of the whole contains a female principle and a male principle. Where some translators rely on the metaphorical possibilities of flora and fauna, she prefers interpretations that are blatantly sexual. (For example, one section, "the night diggers," focuses on pigs that root around in moist and hollowed-out furrows. More traditional translations let them be pigs—and, as such, symbols of both the farmers that prepare soil for a crop and randy men who ravish fertile women. Jensen, though, uses more graphic language, describing not pigs' heads—and therefore human heads—but rather the heads of penises.)

If Jensen takes Hawai'i's foundational text and reimagines it, Kumu Patrick takes it and goes further. And then he reimagines Hawai'i's foundational art form itself. Rather than sticking to Jensen's exact text, he cuts, merges, cuts, and merges her translation of the first eleven sections of the chant. He ends up with distinct story lines depicting the birthing of sea plants and animals, the creating of mountainous islands, the covering of the land with rich flora and fauna, and, finally, the mating of man and woman.

Then he has had to devise rhythms and cadences for a chant that historically was an oli (a vocal chant) and not a mele (a chant meant to be accompanied by dance). "*The Kumulipo* is not parsed out in dance-friendly stanzas," he says.

The choreography relies primarily on hula kahiko, an ancient form of hula known to practitioners, if not to tourists. In keeping with this style, the chants in the first four dances are atonal—not melodic—and are accompanied by a double-gourd drum and, sometimes, a hollowed-out log beaten with bamboo rattles. The costuming is traditional—made of fabric flounced around the waist, poufy for the women, skimpy for the men. The dancers adorn themselves with vines and ferns, nuts and shells. The dancing is primal and athletic, with strong lines and forceful angles.

It's not just the story lines and the movements here that break new hula ground. In the opening multi-media sequence, the sea and the beds of coral are projected onto a huge white scrim behind the dancers. As the story advances, the images projected behind the dancers correspond, loosely, to the creatures featured in the chant. For example, in the second dance come pretty schools of fish, giant manta rays, and tame-looking sharks. Then come the palms and ferns and mosses of the damp forest and "birds that roar and thunder." The lighting changes from gray to peacock blue to green, with accents just bright enough to let flicker the orange and gold hems of the skirts.

In keeping with what's happening thematically, Kumu Patrick varies the texture and tone through choreographic shifts and musical twists. In "Hānau ke Po'o Wa'awa'a" ("Born the Hollowed Furrow"), bare-chested men in *malo,* or loincloths, lean horizontally on the floor, tucking and extending one leg. (The athletic but graceful move is called a *hula 'ōhelo.*) The beat of the *ipu* (gourd drum) is strong, eager, throbbing. The men look like eels, then like amphibians crawling from the swamp, then like something very erotic but hard to name. This is Kumu Patrick's vision of the "night diggers"—that is, the busy, sexy, randy, rooting pigs.

"Hānau ka I'a"

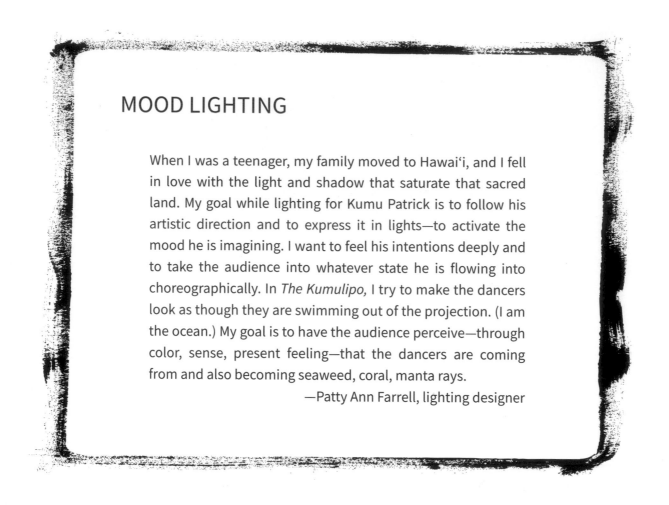

MOOD LIGHTING

When I was a teenager, my family moved to Hawai'i, and I fell in love with the light and shadow that saturate that sacred land. My goal while lighting for Kumu Patrick is to follow his artistic direction and to express it in lights—to activate the mood he is imagining. I want to feel his intentions deeply and to take the audience into whatever state he is flowing into choreographically. In *The Kumulipo,* I try to make the dancers look as though they are swimming out of the projection. (I am the ocean.) My goal is to have the audience perceive—through color, sense, present feeling—that the dancers are coming from and also becoming seaweed, coral, manta rays.

—Patty Ann Farrell, lighting designer

THE LIGHT EMERGES

The last dance takes us to ao, or day, and the mytho-historical time when gods and goddesses are born. This is the era of La'ila'i, Ki'i, and Kāne. The time of mating. The time of women sitting sideways. The time of rubbed firesticks. The time of making multitudes.

The mood changes as the light brightens and the photo montage begins to reflect a world we recognize as our own: a beach, a line of foam from breaking waves, a calm sea. In the distance, two conical islets are silhouetted by a rising sun.

The chanting continues, but it has softened and turned melodic. Under it, and around it, and after it, swells an electronic soundscape composed by DJ and music master Moby. The sound of flutes is followed by distant cries and an occasional echo of "We are the future." It is a plaintive, synthesized melody with an electronic beat. (Think tamped-down timpani, Moog gone rogue.)

A dozen women emerge, dressed in voluminous skirts, their tight bodices made sumptuous by thick lei of a prized mountain vine called *maile.* Their dark hair flows down the back, and their heads are crowned in maile. They dance slowly, gracefully, as if on the cool, hard-packed sand that stretches along the shore.

The light, the music's eerie melancholy, and the lyrical dancing all evoke a whirl of emotions—joy, awe, a tiny bit of fear, a quiet hoping. The chant ends with the words *ua ao, ua ao:* it is the dawn of day, the time of earthly light.

The music continues, though, and more women stream onstage, followed by the men. Soon the stage is full and the entire troupe is dancing in unison, their arms raising overhead in Vs, a multitude of long limbs crisscrossing.

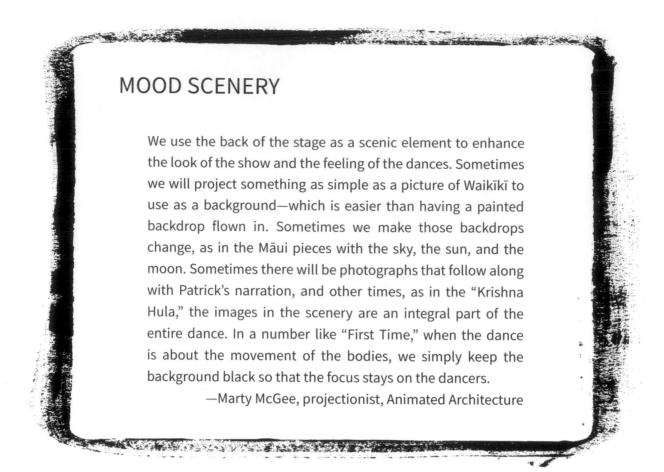

MOOD SCENERY

We use the back of the stage as a scenic element to enhance the look of the show and the feeling of the dances. Sometimes we will project something as simple as a picture of Waikīkī to use as a background—which is easier than having a painted backdrop flown in. Sometimes we make those backdrops change, as in the Māui pieces with the sky, the sun, and the moon. Sometimes there will be photographs that follow along with Patrick's narration, and other times, as in the "Krishna Hula," the images in the scenery are an integral part of the entire dance. In a number like "First Time," when the dance is about the movement of the bodies, we simply keep the background black so that the focus stays on the dancers.

—Marty McGee, projectionist, Animated Architecture

Kumu Patrick, the chanter, lets his voice soften and go melodic. His baritone mixes in and among the liquid chords of Moby. He is invoking the name of Laʻilaʻi, again and again. The scenery changes into a montage of dramatic clouds, swishing swiftly by, superimposed on their own mirror image. Clouds upside-down look strangely like crashing waves, and the viewer has a sense of both knowing and not knowing this sea-sky, but the images fade out, leaving only ambiguity.

Then the sun appears, now large and golden and close, right behind the dancers. The music retreats; the dancers sink onto their knees. All grows still. A baby cries.

It is day. Our world has emerged.

"Ua Ao"

MELE: HAWAIIAN POETIC TEXTS

Hawaiian poetry springs from an ancient tradition among the seafaring Polynesians who established a branch of their society in the Hawaiian Islands around 300 AD. A thousand years of long-distance interaction was followed by centuries of relative isolation, during which the language and poetry of Hawaiians gelled into new forms and styles. The last two centuries have seen especially rapid changes.

Prior to contact with Europeans, Hawaiian poetry was part of a vast oral tradition that ensured social continuity; framed ritual, legends, and genealogy; and documented historical events. Mele, poetic texts or chants, were imbued with sacred power. Those for gods and nobles were seen as manifestations of *mana,* or divine power. Usually intoned in a chant form, poetry was revered in protocols of royal courts and in sacred ceremonies.

In the old, preliterate culture, proper reciting of memorized chants—some hundreds of lines long—was a matter of life and death; this is expressed in the proverb *I ka ʻōlelo nō ke ola, i ka ʻōlelo nō ka make:* "In the word is life, in the word is death." Gods or chiefs might well strike to death a chanter who garbled a chant of ceremonial importance.

The oldest chants petitioned the gods and documented the histories, describing the creation of the world and the genealogical descent of chiefs from the gods. *The Kumulipo* tells of the earth's creation and the genealogical chain of life from coral polyps to the gods and through royal lineages to chief Lono-i-ka-makahiki. In another ancient chant, Kūapākaʻa, keeper of a magic calabash containing the winds, chants the names of ninety-five winds, district by district, including twelve for the single valley of Hālawa on Molokaʻi. The chant *Haui ka Lani,* 809 lines long, is said to be a prophecy of Kamehameha's conquest of the islands.

While poetry was the realm of priests and chiefs, it was also practiced and appreciated by the general population. It was meant to be read aloud, and the chanting of poetry, old or new, became a pleasant pastime. Experts, chiefs, and commoners composed in groups and individually, and new compositions were constantly added to the cultural repertoire. Chants could be composed for the hula, or chanted pieces could be tailored to a metered form that could be presented through the dance.

Whether recited as an invocation, intoned without accompaniment, or presented through dancers as hula, chants expressed the skills of the poet. Composers, though admired, were rarely acknowledged; the inspiration of the poetry—be it person, place, or event—took precedence.

Following Captain Cook's arrival in 1778, continued foreign contact brought a sweep of new cultural influences, and Hawaiian poetry, like the language and culture that framed its existence, was forever altered. Most poetry relating to the ancient religion and to certain ceremonies would be swept away, but the art of composition endured, along with many poetic traditions.

The development of a writing system after 1820 (the Hawaiians had not had a written language) and the rapid embrace of literacy allowed many ancient poems to be recorded in writing. Some chant forms, like *kanikau* (dirges), *mele pai aliʻi* (honorific chants for chiefs), and *mele aloha ʻāina* (place or loyalty chants), were most likely to be published in newspapers. Some chants, and hula chants in general, were considered inappropriate for modern audiences. *Mele nema,* criticizing or defamatory chants, could be slanderously wanton. *Mele maʻi,* or "procreation poems," celebrated the private parts of a newborn, especially those of chiefly rank. The sexual and racy words of such mele, often meant to be performed in dance, were the despair of nineteenth-century missionaries.

Fortunately, chants deemed unseemly for publication in the nineteenth and early twentieth centuries weren't shunned by everyone. Nobles and antiquarians made a pastime of collecting chants of every kind, and some of their compilations, from minimal to massive, survive today in family papers, collections, and various archives, both in Hawaiʻi and abroad.

Mele, the general name for poetry, falls in two main realms: *mele hula,* for the dance, and *mele oli,* for chanting only. *Hīmeni,* from English "hymn," was used for any song not danced to, but the word *mele* eventually slipped into broader common usage to mean "song," so *hīmeni* now generally refers only to Hawaiian hymns.

Musically, chants and songs are very different, yet poetically they are remarkably similar. Melodies, instruments, and song topics have grown in all directions, but much of the poetic structure remains, making modern song the progeny of the ancient chants.

Hawaiian poetry and poetic speech relies on certain devices: imagery and metaphor, reference to storied places or legends, somewhat truncated grammar, embellished forms of words, the linking of lines, and certain types of repetition. The choice and form of these devices is guided and flavored by the *kaona,* or hidden meaning of a poetic piece, often the seed of inspiration that generates and frames a piece of poetry, rather than an encoded message within it.

Although neither uniform line length nor systematic meter is required in Hawaiian poetry, mele composed for hula, especially modern hula, often have fixed meter, regular line length, and discrete verses. Rhyming, however, is avoided in Hawaiian compositions as simplistic, because every word in the language ends in one of five vowels. Instead, lines are linked through a subtle set of conventions, like the repetition of sound, the similarity or opposition of meaning, a question followed by its answer,

(continued on next page)

(continued from previous page)

or a culturally familiar sequence of thought. These clever connective mechanisms also act as mnemonic devices to facilitate the recall of the reciter.

The love of nature is characteristic of Hawaiian poetry, and there is an emphasis on artistic use of natural images. The sea might be called "whispering" (*hāwanawana*), "streaked" (*mā'oki'oki*), or "pebble-rustling" (*nehe i ka 'ili'ili*). A pretty girl is referred to as a flower, a lei, or a soft-eyed surgeonfish (*kole maka onaona*); her back like a cliff and her front like a moon (*pali ke kua, mahina ke alo*). Rains are spread like "a coverlet upon the forest" (*hāli'i i ka nahele*), "lehua-rustling" (*kani lehua*), or "cliff-creeping" (*nihi pali*).

The beautiful imagery of Hawaiian mele, worked within a fabric of poetic devices and careful word selection, elevates the art beyond fine voice or melody and offers layers of enjoyment for anyone who explores there.

—Puakea Nogelmeier, professor of Hawaiian language, University of Hawai'i–Mānoa

"Hānau ke Poʻo Waʻawaʻa"

"Kāwika"

CHAPTER TWO

"Kāwika"

("David")

In the auditorium of Daniel Webster Elementary School on San Francisco's Potrero Hill, hula class begins not so much with a bang as with a *boom-boom*: the sound of two slaps on the side of a large, figure eight–shaped Hawaiian gourd.

Sitting on the floor of the stage, his legs forming a circle around the giant gourd, is a half-Hawaiian Adonis with a shock of dark hair, obsidian eyes, and a deep baritone voice. Yes, this is Kumu Patrick. Facing him are the thirty-odd students of his "sophomore" class, positioned in five staggered rows and ranging in age, hairstyle, body type, and ethnic background. The women wear sweatshirts and gathered cotton *pāʻū* skirts, the men T-shirts and baggy shorts.

Once the warm-up is done, Kumu Patrick jumps up and has the rows move to the back of the room. He is wearing a black T-shirt and board shorts, and his face shows the stubble of a new beard.

"Here's the *hoʻopuka,*" he says, using the name for a quick hula combination, which moves the dancers onto a stage or from the back of the practice room to the front. In this one, the dancers start with a kāholo to the right, then one to the left—

both at a forty-five-degree angle. (The kāholo is hula's most basic step. It's often called a "vamp" and involves a step to the side with the first foot, and a shift of the weight and a brief tap as the second comes to join it, another step to the side with the first foot, and an even briefer tap with the second.) The arms are at chest level, parallel to the floor. One reaches in the direction of the movement; the other stays put in front of the chest.

In tonight's combo, the first two steps to the right angle are taken in an upright stance, the third and fourth are in *'ai ha'a*, a hula plié.

"Up-up-*down*; up-up-*down*," Kumu Patrick demonstrates, his entire body moving like a waving shaft of sugarcane (a very muscular shaft of sugarcane). The next two kāholo are done straight to the right side, then to the left. Describing the movement of the arms and head, he calls out and demonstrates: "Side-side-center; side-side-center." (The right arm extends to the side, then folds back and ends up in front of the chest. The head follows.) "Out and in," he calls, repeating the motion and describing it in a new way.

Then he lets the dancers try the sequence twice, bellowing:

"Up-up-*down*, up-up-*down*,
side-side-center, side-side-center;
up-up-*down*, up-up-*down*,
out and in, out and in."

He pauses and then sends his students back to the starting place. "It's the thinking man's ho'opuka," he says, acknowledging the trickiness of the combination. A few dancers crack half-smiles.

After the ho'opuka comes the first hula of the night, which he calls "Aunti's 'Kāwika.'" It is a softer, sweeter variation on the very first dance he taught these sophomores, who have been studying with him for between four and seven years. He calls that first dance just "Kāwika," and in angular, brawny movements it tells the story of David Kalākaua, the nineteenth-century monarch born to chiefs, beloved by his people, and recognized by the rulers of France and England. (Kāwika, pronounced Kuh-*vee*-kuh, is the transliteration of David.) If a kāholo is the most basic of hula steps, "Kāwika" is the most basic of hula dances.

"When I choreographed *my* 'Kāwika,'" Kumu Patrick stops and explains, "I was just trying to get every motion in there." The idea was to give beginners a transition from warm-up drills to an actual dance. "This version is much older—probably given to Aunti Maiki from Lōkālia," he says, a little reverence softening his voice as he refers to giants in the family hula line. "Back in the old days, hands were held close to the body." He demonstrates, letting his forceful biceps soften and his hands retract a tad. "The vehicle for moving the story was the *words*, not the motions," he explains. "If you are listening to the poetry, the hands just provide a little sweetness."

Kalākaua, whose family line was enumerated in *The Kumulipo*, is honored in every hula class—through this dance or through one of the many others dedicated to him—and for good reason: he was hula's principal patron in the late nineteenth century. But to understand what he did for hula, we need to trace hula's history. (*The Kumulipo* merely explains how we got from the coral polyps to generations of people.) We need to understand the cultural underpinnings of the dance itself and its evolution from primordial times.

"Kalākaua he Inoa"

"Lei Kapa ʻEhu Kai Kaʻena na ka Makani"

ORIGIN STORIES

Hula's Tahitian roots. The high chief Moʻikeha lived in Waipiʻo Valley on the island of Hawaiʻi. Descended from a Tahitian settler, he lived with his brother ʻOlopana and his wife, Luʻukia. When Waipiʻo flooded after a tempest, all three fled to their ancestral home on Raʻiātea. Eventually, Moʻikeha left his family, including a son named Laʻamaikahiki, as well as his prized pahu drum, Hāwea, to return to Hawaiʻi. He settled on Kauaʻi and after some time became king.

Years later, Moʻikeha longed to see Laʻamaikahiki. He sent his Hawaiian-born son, Kila, to Tahiti to find him. Kila was told he would recognize his half-brother by the sound of the drum Hāwea. It was true: Kila heard the sound of the drum on Raʻiātea and met Laʻamaikahiki. The two brothers crossed the ocean together with the drum. As they sailed along the coasts of the islands, Laʻamaikahiki beat the pahu in a distinct pattern. Moʻikeha recognized Laʻamaikahiki from the powerful sound of Hāwea. Upon landing, they were showered with gifts by those who had heard the drumbeats. Later, Laʻamaikahiki went from island to island, teaching the hula and the chants that accompanied the pahu.

Beautiful flower of the beach. A baby girl, born of the union between a goddess and a mortal, was thrown into the sea by her mother, after which a porpoise cow found her and tenderly pushed her to shore. There, at Kahakai, a remote beach on Kauaʻi, woodland spirits raised her. She found shelter under a *hau* tree and learned to sing from a melodious stream. Her friends were the ocean, trees, seabirds, flowers, and the porpoise. She joined them by swaying with the palms, moving like an ocean wave, soaring like a bird. Through the grace of her hands and feet, she became a flower, a rainbow, a waterfall. One day as she danced, the high chief Laʻa saw her, called to her, and succeeded only in sending her back into the woods. When he saw her again, he began to beat a rhythm with his paddle against the side of his canoe. At first she just listened, then she began to sway, and then she danced faster and faster and he accelerated the beat. Finally she fell, spent, and Laʻa paddled to shore, cast his fishnet over her, and took her home to be his wife. He named her Pua-nani-o-ke-Kahakai, "the beautiful flower of Kahakai."

Pele heard about Laʻa's strange bride and plotted Puanani's destruction. She spied on Puanani until she could imitate her and then challenged her to a contest, which many came to watch. Pele's hula was dramatic and earthy. Puanani's was ethereal: she danced with the abandon of a child of the woods and the sea. Puanani won everyone's heart. Pele, enraged, vowed to turn Puanani to stone but decided on a palm tree instead. As soon as she transformed Puanani, a breeze caught the top of the tree, and the fronds

began to dance like the fingers and arms of Puanani. The strong, supple trunk swayed. To this day, dancers look to the coconut palm dancing in the wind as a model of hula motion. (This account is adapted from *Hula Is Life*.)

Stories of Laka. Throughout the islands, dancers revere Laka as the divinity of dance. She is the goddess of the hula, of the fragrant vine *maile ʻieʻie*, and of other forest plants. In one origin story, two gods of hula, a male and a female, came to Hawaiʻi from Tahiti and showed Hawaiians how to dance and chant. They both claimed credit for creating the dance, so, to settle the argument, they competed, chanting and dancing from dawn to dusk. They danced with such intensity that their bodies became one. In the end, only the hula goddess Laka remained.

In other myths, Laka was a male god and hula honored virility as well as intensity. (The dance, it was said, provided physical conditioning and helped prepare warriors for battle. Some dances still contain movements that reflect fighting poses.) According to this line of thought, Laka taught the volcano goddess Pele's youngest sister, Hiʻiaka, how to dance, and women joined in the tradition. Over time, Hiʻiaka became the greatest patroness of the hula, with hundreds of dances dedicated to her.

The most well-known *heiau*, or temple, for hula dancers is below Kēʻē cliff in Hāʻena, Kauaʻi. It is dedicated to Laka and carries the name Ka Ulu o Laka.

THE ANCIENT STORY

The story of hula starts in the realm of mythology and legend. According to many myths, the powerful, provocative dance is said to have originated with the goddess Laka, who is identified with hula, fertility, the forest, and various blossoms and ferns. Some accounts suggest she was a kind of two-in-one figure, a real person as well as a goddess.

In traditional schools of hula, an altar for Laka was set up in the hālau. (The word *hālau* literally means "longhouse" or "meetinghouse," where, traditionally, people would gather for instruction on canoe making, hula, or other arts. Today, *hālau* is translated mostly as "school.") Before the altar, students pray to Laka for inspiration. Laka figures in many chants that are still performed, and the contemporary hula dancer must find a way to bring Laka's ambiguous presence to life in order to invest power and meaning in the dance.

"I think of Laka as the forest—the *palai*, the *ʻieʻie*, the *lehua,* all the wonderful ferns and flowers," says Kumu Patrick. "She is a powerful expression of nature. Today most hālau—including mine—don't have a *kuahu*, an altar we adorn with foliage from the forest. It's as if we've taken to wearing the greenery on our bodies so Laka can inhabit and inspire us that way."

There are many accounts of hula's beginnings—some involving Laka, others not. People of different islands once subscribed to different myths about the origin of the dance:

- On the island of Hawaiʻi, it was believed that Hiʻiaka danced the first hula in honor of her older sister Pele.
- On Molokaʻi and Oʻahu, the famous voyager Laʻamaikahiki is said to have brought the first drums to Hawaiʻi around 1000 AD; then he taught the dance to people of the Hawaiian Islands.
- Also on Oʻahu, two women were said to have danced the first hula in a fierce competition for the same lover (the competition took place during a game of *kilu*, a pastime of chiefs comparable to our modern culture's traditional kissing games, but a step more erotic; it included exhibitions of dance and song that called for the highest development of skill in these arts).
- And on Kauaʻi, the goddess Kilinoe was the preeminent hula mistress.

THE MORE MODERN STORY

Though we honor many of these gods, goddesses, and other personages in our hula lineage, our understanding of the dance remains murky until the nineteenth century, when Westerners arrived and started making drawings and paintings of it. But even that knowledge is incomplete, since it was frequently shaped by the attitudes of the missionaries and settlers who made them.

Scholars are still piecing together the role and form of ancient dancing, from new archives and even from sources like early-nineteenth-century newspapers. Here is some of what they've found: Hula was the history book of a people without a written language. Dance was accompanied by the beating of sharkskin drums, gourds, sticks, and pebbles. Gestures were secondary to chanted poetry. Hula chants were the sacred text maintaining the relationship between gods and mortals, heralding chiefs, celebrating sex, and tracing the subtleties of the natural world, whether the steepness of volcanic cliffs or the variety of mists that clung to them.

When Calvinist missionaries arrived in the Hawaiian Islands in 1820, the hula they encountered was primal and powerful. Scandalized, the missionaries opposed the dance and tried to suppress it, letting the ruling chiefs know about their disdain. Eventually the Hawaiian legislature passed civil codes regulating its performance. Hula was driven underground, practiced discreetly within families or in the far corners of the islands.

Then, half a century later, hula found its savior in King Kalākaua, who viewed it as "the heartbeat of the Hawaiian people." He revived the dance, combining ancient elements of poetry and chant with new instruments and costumes.

David Laʻamea Kamanakapuʻu Mahinulani Nāleiaʻehuokalani Lumialani Kalākaua (the king's full name) ruled the Hawaiian kingdom from 1874 until his death in 1891 and cut a figure Shakespeare would have loved. Think Hawaiian Falstaff—erudite, ribald, proud, and "party hardy." Both his critics then and his partisans now called him the Merrie Monarch, and he came by the moniker honestly. Critics cite his political weakness and bad decisions, but as a cultural force he was indeed merry and monumental. He and his brother and sisters were known as Nā Lani ʻEhā ("The Royal Four") for their musical talents, and he sponsored glee clubs, choral groups, and the Royal Hawaiian Band. He championed the then-new ʻukulele and choreographed dances. He gathered experts at his court, collected artifacts, elevated hula, and encouraged the practice of traditional arts—whether the Hawaiian martial art of lua, the sport of surfing, or the reciting of genealogical chants like *The Kumulipo*. He was famous for parties at his boathouse, Healani, but he also showcased hula on the palace grounds.

Kalākaua didn't do all this just out of love for his culture. He was intentionally defying the abstemious missionaries by fortifying his own rule, stoking pride among his subjects, and offering a new national narrative. For his coronation in 1883, Kalākaua brought kumu hula and their hālau from the countryside and neighbor-

King David Kalākaua

ing islands. At his fiftieth-birthday jubilee in 1886, as many as sixty people performed at a time—chanting, singing newly composed tunes, and dancing rare temple hula, as well as newer hula forms, which blended Western and Hawaiian music and dance vocabularies.

A number of women received formal hula training in Kalākaua's court. Among the best known is Jennie Wilson (Kini Kapahu), who, with other former court dancers, went on to spread the knowledge of hula across America and Europe. These "hula girls" performed in international expositions, vaudeville theaters, dime museums, and royal courts, reminding Westerners that Hawaiians were a distinct people with their own sacred and secular culture. (See chapter eight for more on Jennie Wilson and the hula girls.)

ANCIENT HULA

In pre–Western contact Hawaiian society, *ha'a* referred to ritual movements performed for gods at temples. *Hula*, performed to specific chants, referred to dances performed for a human audience in a nonsacred context. Dancers maintained a low, bent-knee stance called *'ai ha'a*, and steps were beaten out by gourds, drums, or other percussion instruments, like stones and bamboo rattles.

After the arrival of Europeans, sacred traditions were forced underground and Western influence affected Hawaiian hula. Terms used to describe hula shifted and merged, and new ones appeared. By the middle of the twentieth century, *kahiko* became the general term to classify "ancient" or "old" styles, and *'auana* became the general term to describe "modern" or newer styles. Following are some classifications of kahiko used by scholars and hālau today, though not all *po'e hula*, or "people of hula," agree on the definitions.

Hula kuahu: This general term refers to sacred hula performed under the protection of the goddess Laka and in accordance with certain rituals. *Kuahu* means "altar"; an altar to Laka or other hula deities would be set up and maintained throughout teaching or dancing.

Danse des hommes dans les îles Sandwich

Hula pahu: Here, choreography is accompanied by the pahu drum, an instrument reserved for only the most sacred mele. These dances were taught in hālau, and the repertoire was religious, often honoring *akua* (gods). Chiefs claimed items of repertoire, however, in order to assert genealogical descent from those gods. The scholar Adrienne Kaeppler says that before 1819, "the term for hula performed in conjunction with wooden drums was *hula kā'eke*, but with the secularization of objects associated with temples, such performances eventually became known as hula pahu."

Hula 'āla'apapa: These dances performed to the accompaniment of an ipu heke (double gourd) evolved from hula of the pre–Western contact era that was performed outside of temple rituals. *Hula 'āla'apapa* still honored gods, though, and is closely associated with hula kuahu.

Hula 'ōlapa: Like hula 'āla'apapa, this style is accompanied by an ipu heke. Contrary to its designation as an "ancient" form, *hula 'ōlapa* developed during the late monarchy period. This style is set apart from hula 'āla'apapa by the more standardized length and phrasing of the chants and the more secular subject matter. (These dances typically pay tribute to chiefs and royalty.) Some say that *hula 'ōlapa* is a shortened form of *'āla'apapa*. *'Ōlapa* can also refer to a dancer or group of dancers.

WANDERING HULA

During Kalākaua's era, some dances were still viewed as sacred and practiced only in hālau by the truly initiated. But under the king's auspices, elements of Hawaiian poetry, chant, dance, and costuming merged with those of the West to create a new, hybrid form, *hula ku'i*, which literally means "dance combining old and new." Some hula ku'i steps were even derived from ballroom dances like the minuet.

Over time, as hula kept evolving, the names of different genres also evolved. Hula 'auana, which literally means "wandering hula," came to be used for modern dances that evolved out of the hula ku'i of the monarchy years. These hula often praise aspects of a modern, secular world: the diamond ring of a queen, the "famous firemen" of Honolulu, or a favorite spot for lovers in Victorian-era Waikīkī.

"Hilo One," a hula 'auana taught in many Nā Lei Hulu i ka Wēkiu classes, combines the sweet and the sassy. Composed in 1894, it refers to the part of Hilo, stretching along a black-sand beach, that was home to Emalia Kaihumua, another of Kalākaua's court dancers. She is called "sweet Emalia" in the dance, and her charms, we're told, include coy and teasing looks, often cast in the direction of suitors who appear in metaphorical form in the song. First we learn of the *liko*, or tender bud—a stand-in for a young, attractive man. Then there is the *i'iwi polena*, the scarlet honeycreeper that lives in the uplands, indiscriminately flying from tree to tree. Finally, we get a mysterious Henry, who may or may not be either of these.

"Ho'okahi 'Oi o ke Kaona"

"Hilo One"

Emalia "haunts the thoughts" of the composer, who is pained by a love "rooted deep in the bones." It seems to be a little soap opera in a song, or at least a love triangle involving the sweet but mischievous Emalia, the honest but jilted composer, and the attractive Henry, with his tendency to flit from flower to flower. Henry gets the girl, but the composer hasn't given up. The point of the poetry is to convince Emalia that he is actually the best bud.

The dance itself is lively and fast. The dancers must embody Emalia, with her mischievous looks and lighthearted affections, but they must also pick and protect the tender bud and move with the fleetness and daring of the scarlet bird.

By contrast, dancing a hula kahiko, literally "old or ancient dance," is a more serious, though not sober, affair. This more traditional genre is accompanied by percussive instruments and chanting. Some hula kahiko are secular, honoring chiefs or praising particular places (though even these chants may end with a dedication to the gods). Although they look backward in content and style, many were composed in the nineteenth and twentieth centuries.

Many kahiko trace mythological stories and legends. One example, "No Luna i ka Hale Kai," captures a moment in Hiʻiaka's journey across the islands to fetch a handsome young man from Kauaʻi for her sister Pele back on Hawaiʻi Island. The poetry offers a swooping, zoom-lens description of Puna, Hawaiʻi. It also looks close up at Hōpoe, the lehua-woman who fears the predations of blossom-hungry men. (The lehua blossom is usually the first flower to appear on a new lava flow.) And it describes rough surf as it rattles the beach pebbles and echoes in pandanus groves.

MODERN HULA

When Calvinist missionaries arrived in the Hawaiian Islands in 1820, they quickly denounced the hula as heathen. And, with the support of recently converted chiefs and the queen regent, Ka'ahumanu, it was driven underground. But after a fifty-year period of dormancy, King David Kalākaua celebrated the hula, knowing that it would be essential in shoring up a culture battered by European and American influence.

He and others wrote new songs that retained the essence of Hawaiian poetry but were arranged into stanzas and influenced by Western tempos like waltz and polka. (Two of the most famous were written by Kalākaua and his sister, who became Queen Lili'uo-kalani. They are "Hawai'i Pono'ī," which is the state song today, and "Aloha 'Oe," a love song that came to be known throughout the islands and the world.) Softening the urgent beat of earlier hula, guitar, piano, bass, and 'ukulele were enlisted to accompany Hawaiian percussion instruments like the gourd drum, feather-decorated gourd rattles, split-bamboo rattles, stomped sticks, and stone castanets.

These changes brought about new forms of hula:

Hula ku'i: *Ku'i* means "to join, stitch, splice, or unite," and the hula of Kalākaua's era stitched together the musical and dance vocabularies of old with new elements from indigenous and Western cultures. The dance became more secular and less rooted in Hawaiian spirituality.

Hula 'auana: In the decades following the overthrow of the Hawaiian monarchy, hula continued to incorporate Western melodies and instruments, as well as contemporary stories and dress. The term *'auana*, meaning "to wander," initially described hula that was not restricted by religious prayer and ritual. Eventually, *'auana* came to refer to the graceful, sensuous, and playful "modern" hula, and *hula ku'i* to the hula of Kalākaua's era.

The genre hula kahiko has come to include another type of hula, called hula pahu, which is named for the sharkskin drum and considered especially sacred. It also includes many *hula ma'i*, the lusty class of dances that promote procreation. For example, the message in the hula "Kō Ma'i 'Ulu Hua" is imparted through separate verses describing the picking, washing, cooking, smelling, devouring, and savoring of the *'ulu*, or breadfruit, but the lyrics and movements resound with double entendres: the delectable 'ulu is a stand-in for an exquisite lover.

"Eia ʻo Nāleiaʻehu"

"No Luna i ka Halekai"

TO YOU, O SHINING SUN

For all that King Kalākaua had done for hula and Hawaiian culture, when he died in San Francisco in 1891, he took with him a bit of the cultural ebullience he had fostered. His sister, Queen Liliʻuokalani, moved onto the throne after his death, but in trying to shore up some of the power her brother had ceded to them, she ran afoul of a crowd of missionary sons, American settlers, and white merchants eager for stronger ties with the United States. In a sham revolution in 1893, planned by leaders of this group, the queen was overthrown. Ultimately, annexation—or, as some writers and speakers now prefer, "occupation"—along with the modernization of the twentieth century, proved devastating to hula.

In 1896, English replaced Hawaiian as the language of the government, the courts, and the schools. English became the lingua franca, eventually replacing Hawaiian in everything from advertising to conversations at the dinner table. And in 1898, Hawaiʻi became a territory of the United States. The political power of the Hawaiian people was suppressed. One sign of this suppression was that the more ancient and sacred forms of hula went underground and were taught only within some families and a few hālau, or they vanished. Soon radio and television replaced traditional entertainment. Hollywood and tourism presented a bastardized form of Hawaiian dance to the world that had nothing to do with true hula kahiko or ʻauana. By the time Hawaiʻi became a state in 1959, modernization had fully moved in. Hula—along with slack-key guitar, traditional methods of fishing, navigating by the stars, and composing in the Hawaiian language— was on the wane.

But then came the Hawaiian Cultural Renaissance in the 1970s, when Native Hawaiians (either living on the islands or spread out by the diaspora) started to self-consciously revive the things that were slipping away. They took a renewed interest in traditional practices, including hula. The old idea that music, dance, and chanting were not just entertainment but had the power to make political and cultural statements took hold once again.

For many, the first sign that something new was afoot was an album called *Guava Jam*, which was released by a trio of young musicians (a guitarist, a bassist, and an ʻukulele wizard) who called themselves The Sunday Mānoa. They used every traditional instrument in the Hawaiian arsenal but wrote music that had a rock beat and a youthful sense of urgency. The album hit radio stations in 1971 and brought the music of luaus and family gatherings to a younger audience.

The first and most popular track was a brash reimagining of "Kāwika," the century-old paean to King Kalākaua. The 1971 song starts with the simple beat of an ipu and then adds one traditional Hawaiian instrument after another, including stones and a bamboo rattle. Then an ʻukulele plays a riff, traveling to all reaches of the fretboard, using double stops, hammer-ons, pull-offs, and the occasional sweep to keep the music sizzling. Guitars join in, the percussion fades out, and the rich harmonies begin. The music is at once completely traditional and completely new.

Most hula dancers know more than one version of "Kāwika"—not to mention other songs for or about the Merrie Monarch. One of the latter is "Iā ʻOe e ka Lā" ("To You, o Shining Sun"), which was composed in 1881 to celebrate King Kalākaua's circumnavigation of the globe. He was the first monarch in the world to accomplish the feat, and in the song he is called a light that illuminates Hawaiʻi and the rest of the world. Various choral groups have recorded this song, singing in four-part harmonies and backed by all manner of instruments.

For years, Kumu Patrick taught his students an ʻauana version, but he has come to prefer a kahiko version choreographed by Aunti Maiki Aiu Lake. For this version he turns off the stereo, picks up an ipu heke,

Patrick Makuakāne dancing at 'Ōhikilolo Ranch, in the early 1980s.

and sings the melody himself. "This is an old dance in our repertoire," he tells his Wednesday night junior class. "It's simple and, well, beautiful. I just love it."

He stands barefoot on the cafeteria stage and reviews the context of the song. It describes Kalākaua's 1881 journey around the world. The king, Kumu Patrick explains, wanted to establish diplomatic relations with other nations and to convince workers from Asia and Europe to come to Hawai'i to work in the sugarcane fields. Also, imagining his own kingdom on the world stage, he just wanted to observe the leaders of these countries and seek models for his own reign.

"Kalākaua was interested in the trappings of the aristocracy," Kumu Patrick tells his students, facetiously invoking famous portraits of the king in Western-style jackets with epaulets, ribbons, and lots of decoration. "All those shiny buttons, satin sashes, extravagant medallions."

Kumu Patrick launches into the first verse: "*Iā 'oe e ka lā e 'alohi nei 'eā/ Ma nā welelau, ma nā welelau a'o ka honua*" ("To you, o sun shining down/ Rays reaching down to all the ends of the world"). He sets down his ipu heke and extends both arms to the right side, at chest level, reaching toward a corner of the room at a forty-five-degree angle. "Make a nice sun," he calls out, "not a droopy sun." Slowly and intentionally, he lets his hands rise to form a circle overhead, with thumbs and forefingers almost touching.

In the 'auana version these dancers learned as beginners, the arms are straight, the visage serious, the movement swift. But this version, Kumu Patrick says, "should be nice and fluffy. See?" In the next sequence, the hands fall, one at a time making the sun's rays. "Go, sun rays, go!" he calls out.

Then he focuses on the footwork. "Remember, this is Aunti's dance, so the 'uehe lifts up." He continues talking as he demonstrates Aunti's version of a move in which the knees usually pop to the sides. "Lift that foot up, then bring it down. Do not slide it. It's like pedaling backwards on a bicycle. And keep your hips moving!"

Next, he tries to draw the right facial expressions out of his dancers, who are wearing the knit brows and scowls of people who are concentrating deeply on a new dance—one in which the words are in a foreign language and the movements are far from those you'd see on a typical dance floor.

"The stones on your face are weighing you down," Kumu Patrick teases. "I know, I know; you're saying to yourself, 'I'm just trying to learn this frickin' dance.' But so what? I mean, you're going around the world with KK! You mess up, and we make an emergency stop in Berlin." Students laugh under their breath and show a bit of hilarity in their glances at each other.

He continues in this vein for another of the song's eight verses. "In this verse, the cliffs hold secrets," he says. "There's a little bit of a lean as you go seeking for the cliff. Then there is a dig. . . ." He demonstrates how the body straightens and how each arm plunges next to the hip, digging downward, circling to the front of the body, and carving, with the other arm, a wide crater. "Soften it a bit. Relax and have fun."

He continues to coach, cajole, tease, laugh, mime, and demand grace from his students. After several run-throughs, he lets them rest for a few seconds. "Not too shabby-alababby," he says, and smiles. "Remember, I want this fluffy and full of joy!"

"Ki'eki'e e nā Hana a ka Lani"

A hula honoring Aunti Maiki

CHAPTER THREE

"Pua Līlīlehua"

("Red Sagebrush Flower")

Genealogies are almost as important in hula as they are in chiefly lines. Dancers in a hālau learn the repertoire of their hula line, as well as a particular movement style. Certain practices, too, are handed down for generations, from master to disciple—whether how to prepare an altar for the goddess Laka or how to learn by watching and imitating (and *not* by asking questions).

In the case of Kumu Patrick and his hālau, everything flows from a groundbreaking teacher named Aunti Maiki Aiu Lake. Her work over more than three decades earned her the moniker Mother of the Hawaiian Renaissance, but that only begins to express her influence. It started with her dances: many she received from her own teachers, but some she choreographed herself to new songs that were written for her. It was further expressed in her distinctive movement style—fluid, funny, sometimes understated, always lovely. But mostly her influence was felt because she revolutionized the way in which hula was passed on to later generations. Having herself studied with the most important teachers of her day, she codified a modern way of teaching the hula in classes. And she developed a way of grooming new teachers in the esoteric rituals of hula. In her lifetime, she trained forty-two kumu hula, including the three key teachers in Kumu Patrick's life.

When Margaret "Maiki" Souza was born in Honolulu in 1925, hula had effectively been driven underground. Those who kept it alive did so mostly within their own extended families. It was within one of those families, in Pauoa Valley, that Maiki herself took her first tentative hula steps, under the watchful eyes of the mothers and grandmothers of cousins and friends. The young Maiki attended Saint Francis Convent School, boarding there after her adoptive parents died. In high school, she and some schoolmates, along with a hula-dancing cousin, formed a Hawaiian Club and put on shows featuring hula in the 'auana style, the common dances that flourished after the monarchy period and became staples of the tourist industry. The girls would also dance at Kilohana Gardens in Kāne'ohe and Queen's Surf in Waikīkī. Maiki had a tinkling laugh, danced the comic hula, and kept the other girls organized.

One day, her adopted sister began to talk about meeting a female probation officer who taught hula pahu, the once-sacred form of dance that Christians frowned upon and had driven underground. That teacher was Lōkālia Montgomery, a renowned chanter and

Margaret "Maiki" Souza

dancer. Maiki and two others secretly took a bus to Montgomery's house on Charles Street in Kapahulu, a residential and commercial district that lies *mauka*, or "toward the mountains," from Waikīkī.

Montgomery's students have remembered her as stern and strict but also gentle-hearted. She taught in her home and in the style of her own teachers. Students learned by watching, listening, and imitating, and they were neither given translations nor permitted to take notes. Hula heavyweights, including the scholar Mary Kawena Pukui and the dancer Sally Moanikeala Wood, visited the classes.

Much of the advanced teaching was done one-on-one, in a "talk story" format. Certain students, like Maiki, were put through a very special training regimen, and then the best of those students were elevated to special statuses in a formal graduation ceremony known as an *ʻūniki*. (One Hawaiian dictionary suggests that the term is probably related to *niki*, "to tie," since knowledge was thought to be "bound" to the graduated student.) Montgomery anointed Maiki to the status of 'ōlapa, or dancer. Even though she was already performing professionally, Maiki decided she wanted to learn more—not just about hula but also about her Hawaiian heritage. For that, she turned to her kumu's kumu, Kawena Pukui, who was by then considered the foremost twentieth-century expert on Hawaiian customs and language.

"Maiki spent many hours visiting Kawena," recalls Pukui's daughter, Pat Namaka Bacon. "They would talk about anything that came up—hula, music, anything that popped into Kawena's head.

"Maiki was good at storytelling," Bacon continues. "She made the story come alive. She was like Kawena that way. She could be such fun. And she could be serious. The two of them really got along." The sympathy between the two allowed Pukui to trust Maiki with more recondite information, Bacon adds, especially because Pukui worried that "the older things" were dying out and would not otherwise be passed on. "Maiki had

Aunti Maiki's tradition of 'ūniki continues with Papa 'Ūniki Laua'e 2003, under the direction of Kumu Hula Mae Klein.

seen different practices, but nobody had explained them to her or given her any reasons [for them]," Bacon explains. "She came to us because our interest in hula was for preservation, not entertainment. What Maiki learned from Kawena, she would impart to her students."

MOTHER OF THE HAWAIIAN RENAISSANCE

Eventually, Maiki earned the highest 'ūniki status: teacher. (The term *kumu*, which literally means "source" or "foundation," came back into vogue later as a synonym for a teacher who had gone through the traditional 'ūniki training.) In the meantime, she had also married Boniface Aiu, had a few children, and, in 1946, opened her own school, called Margaret Aiu's Hula Studio.

A cultural renaissance soon swept the Hawaiian Islands, infused with ethnic pride. Worried that knowledge was slipping away as times changed and the Hawaiian language was no longer being spoken in homes, Maiki developed a pioneering method of teaching that included not just dance steps but also genealogy, culture, mannerisms, legends, poetry, and the arts and crafts of Hawai'i. Her students recorded these lessons on paper, collected in loose-leaf notebooks.

Kumu Hula Mae Klein

Hula is life," Aunti Maiki was fond of saying. "It expresses everything we see, feel, hear, smell, taste, and touch." Generations of kumu hula in her line have repeated this aphorism, including Aunti Mae Klein, shown above, who has carried on the ʻūniki practice of her kumu and graduated Kumu Patrick in 2003.

"Hawai'i is hula, and hula is Hawai'i," Maiki said when asked to define the dance that was at the center of her life. "The history, the culture, the biographies of the people, descriptions of the island, chronicles of events, messages of love and thanks, or scoldings—all this and more is told in the hula that were danced long ago and that are danced today."

Over time, the school grew, changed locations, and grew some more. Eventually, Maiki changed its name to Hālau Hula o Maiki, becoming the first teacher in many years to use the term *hālau*. The change reflected her own interest in traditional practices, but it also showed one of the many small ways in which she was a pioneer. Within a generation, the "hula studios" of the early twentieth century had been replaced by other hālau. Maiki was a model for other teachers equally committed to the deep traditions of hula.

Aunti Maiki embodied a mix of many

The Sunday Mānoa: Robert Cazimero, Peter Moon, and Roland Cazimero in the 1970s.

qualities. Talk to her former students, and you will hear them describe her as everything from humble to headstrong, curious to kind. Some mention unconditional love, others Catholic devotion. But one thing they all agree on is her fundamental charisma. "To see her, to hear her—there was some kind of magic," says Aunti Mae Klein, a student and protégée. "From day one in 1954, I said, 'I'm not leaving this woman.'" She struggles to find one word that expresses the essence of Maiki's pull, and then settles on it: "compassion."

Puakea Nogelmeier, a professor of Hawaiian language at the University of Hawai'i–Mānoa, who was also one of Maiki's students, describes a similar trait. "She could be stern, but I never heard her raise her voice. I never heard her be negative. She killed it with *aloha*."

Maiki's nurturing personality earned her the sobriquet Mother of the Hawaiian Renaissance.

Among the pages in the notebooks of Kumu Patrick's students at Nā Lei Hulu i ka Wēkiu are the lyrics and interpretations of many of the songs associated with this hula great-grandmother. Some of them are traditional kahiko, like "No Luna i ka Hale Kai," mentioned previously, and "Kaulīlua." The latter compares Mt. Wai'ale'ale, on the island of Kaua'i, to a woman. "Doubly cold is Mount Wai'ale'ale," it begins, "whose eyes peer down on the stunted lehua." Aunti Maiki once explained the chant's meaning: "You know how when women love, they allow you to come close, and when they don't want you, they keep you away? The mountain is like that. It exposes itself when it wants you to approach its beauty, and when it doesn't want you, then it shrouds itself in mist."

Other dances Kumu Patrick and his students have inherited are an ode to a king, "Kāwika"; an ode to a place, "Pua 'Āhihi"; and an ode to Maiki herself, "Pua Līlīlehua." The latter is a dance composed for Maiki by the singer Kahauanu Lake, her third husband. The *līlīlehua* is the red sagebrush flower. It is also the name of

John Keola Lake was an authority on Hawaiian language, religion, oral traditions, and protocol. He was also one of the official *kahu*, or priests, of the City and County of Honolulu—which meant he blessed buildings, prayed for postal workers, and performed weddings. He was *kahuna nui* ("chief priest") at Puʻukoholā Heiau and an advisor to the National Park Service.

the wind and rain in Pālolo Valley, where Maiki lived, and the name of a legendary maiden who resided in the valley and who was courted by a *moʻo*, or magic lizard-dragon. The music is lilting and so pretty it is almost sad. A favorite among Nā Lei Hulu dancers, the dance is slow, the gestures soft and infinitely loving.

HULA GUYZ

In the early 1970s, Maiki took the unprecedented step of opening a class to train students to become teachers themselves. She even advertised it in the newspaper, flouting the traditional practice of trusting only members of the extended family to carry on a hula line. The first kumu hula graduated in 1972; over the next eleven years, she graduated forty-one more. Three Maiki-trained kumu hula laid the foundations for San Francisco's Nā Lei Hulu i ka Wēkiu: John Keola Lake, Robert Uluwehi Cazimero, and Mae Kamāmalu Klein.

John Keolamakaʻāinanakalahuiokalaniokamehamehaekolu Lake began teaching at St. Louis School, in Honolulu, in 1962. Soon he evolved from an academic with an impressive name and impressive credentials in the Spanish language to the teacher who established the first Hawaiian-language class in the state of Hawaiʻi, in 1965. He had learned at the knees of his grandmother and aunties and had gone on to study hula under various masters before seeking out Aunti Maiki. (John Keola Lake was also a cousin and adopted brother of Kahauanu Lake.) As interest in Hawaiian culture surged, he developed a Hawaiian-studies program at the boys' preparatory school. Soon he was teaching academic classes in music and dance, too, and his hula club, Hui o nā ʻŌpio, boasted three hundred students. One of those was Kumu Patrick, then a freshman at St. Louis.

Kumu Patrick says his first experience of hula—in fifth grade, at the Kamehameha School's Exploration program, where ten-year-olds from all over the islands gathered for immersion in Hawaiian culture—did not exactly mark him as a kumu in the making, or even a dancer-to-be. "The whole experience of being with other young Hawaiian kids—swimming, learning Hawaiian words, playing *ulu maika*, a traditional Hawaiian pitching game, was great. But the one class I hated was hula. The instructor wasn't very nice, and he was a big, flaming *māhū* [gay]. Now I recognize that I was grappling with the complicated issue of my own sexuality," Kumu Patrick continues. "The confidence with which he expressed his flamboyance frightened me. Now, of course, I consider that one of his most endearing qualities."

But at St. Louis High School in 1975, Hawaiian culture was cool and Hui o nā ʻŌpio was "the thing to do," especially for a freshman with a name like Patrick Makuakāne and an interest in Hawaiian music. In fact, when Lake asked his students in the first class why they were there, Kumu Patrick answered innocently, "Learn Hawaiian songs." Mr. Lake made his opinion of that quite clear: "He told me, 'If you want to join, you have to sing and dance. If you don't like it, there's the door,'" Kumu Patrick explains. "He was intimidating but still *ʻoluʻolu*, super nice."

It didn't take long for the reluctant student to come around. After two weeks, Kumu Patrick was "hooked on hula," he says, and he credits the man he still calls "Mr. Lake" for his transformation. Kumu Patrick had grown up in Kaimukī, a district of Honolulu. His father is pure Hawaiian, from a Hawaiʻi Island family, and his mother is pure Pennsylvanian, but Kumu Lake is the one who made the biracial boy interested in his culture. "He *was* that Renaissance Hawaiian man," Kumu Patrick says. "He fully embodied every role. I remember thinking, 'I want to do this for the rest of my life.'"

If Kumu Lake got him started, others kept him going. During his sophomore year, Kumu Patrick saw a performance by an all-male troupe, Robert Cazimero's troupe Nā Kamalei o Līlīlehua. "I was amazed," Kumu Patrick remembers today. "They were a combination of Joe Namath and Gene Kelly—graceful, powerful, stunning, athletic, subtle, masculine, all at once." He and two friends worked up the nerve to approach Cazimero, a renowned entertainer who performed with his brother Roland at the Prow Lounge in the Sheraton Waikīkī.

Though his career as a kumu hula was just beginning, Robert Cazimero had already made a mark on Hawaiian music. At eighteen, he and his jam-session buddy (and guitar-ʻukulele-banjo wizard) Peter Moon conscripted his older brother Roland Cazimero for a new band named The Sunday Mānoa. Their first album, *Guava Jam*, helped spark the Hawaiian Renaissance. Robert Cazimero had been dancing for years—first, in his musical family's Polynesian shows (he was the tenth of twelve children), and later at Kamehameha School, where he studied hula for two years with Winona "Aunty Nona" Beamer, a champion of authentic Hawaiian culture as well as an author and composer.

Years later, sitting in the penthouse common room of a Makiki apartment building, looking out toward Diamond Head, Robert Cazimero reflects on the way Aunty Nona and her cousin Mahi influenced his own hula style. "The type of movement, the hips, the feeling—it's Beamer style," he says. "The first time I saw Mahi Beamer

Known as an innovating kumu hula, Robert Cazimero is proud of his own hula roots. "Even to this day," he says, "no accolades—lei, trophies, honors, awards—are as meaningful to me as someone saying, 'You dance like Aunti Maiki Aiu Lake.'" (He is shown here with Aunti Maiki Aiu Lake.)

dance, I saw that a male hula dancer could be comfortable, empowered. *Waiho ka hilahila mai ka hale e hula*—'leave the shame at home and dance!'" he adds. (This is an abbreviation of a proverb known to many dancers: *'A'a i ka hula, waiho ka hilahila i ka hale*, or, "When one wants to dance the hula, bashfulness should be left at home.")

It was also in Nona Beamer's class that Cazimero first met Aunti Maiki, though it was a few years before he joined her Papa 'Ūniki Lehua class and graduated as a kumu hula in 1973. Maiki embraced the importance of the male hula dancer, maintaining that men were central to the understanding of the dance. Her hālau was the first school in many years to graduate male kumu hula, and she let it be known that she harbored a dream that one of them would start an all-male hālau.

In 1975, Cazimero did just that, founding Hālau Nā Kamalei o Līlīlehua with a dream of his own. "When I started teaching my guys, I didn't want them to dance like me, because I dance like my kumu, who had a lovely, flowing style. I wanted them to be graceful but manly." He says the fierce competition among some of his early athletic dancers—including Kumu Patrick—partly dictated that style.

The group made waves from the get-go. After decades of Hollywood images of girls in grass skirts and coconut bras, Cazimero helped shift perceptions of what hula should, and could, be. His men were mature, handsome, and virile. They danced at the Royal Hawaiian's Monarch Room in the 1980s; the Waikīkī Shell in the 1980s, 1990s, and aughts; and the Merrie Monarch's fiftieth-anniversary *hōʻike* (festival) in 2013—not to mention numerous other venues in between. The choreography was daring, the dancing surprising. Cazimero integrated modern dance and hula, even calling the highly visual productions "ballet kahiko."

"I love Balanchine," Cazimero says. "I used to go through ballet books and look at the poses, the hands, the costumes. Maiki was an innovator, too, so I came to this honestly."

"He was young, talented, brash, controversial," Kumu Patrick notes when asked about Cazimero's influence on him. "He was integrating other music and dance into his repertoire. He was really pushing the boundaries."

SAN FRANCISCO KUMU

Cazimero expresses no surprise that Kumu Patrick would himself push boundaries. "He was part of a group of guys—whippersnappers, real firecrackers," Cazimero says about his protégé. "I first saw it when we were dancing at the Royal Hawaiian. And when it came time to step up, he stepped up."

As it turned out, that time came almost as soon as Kumu Patrick relocated to San Francisco in 1984 to pursue a degree in physical education at San Francisco State. He got the degree and spent fifteen years as a personal trainer, but he hardly gave up hula. In fact, he started teaching a handful of dancers within a year of his arrival in the city, in a studio on Sanchez Street, near the Castro. One of his students brought along her seven-year-old. One day he asked the child, "Baby, do you want to come try?" That seven-year-old is now one of his company performers, Makani da Silva, as well as a teacher in his children's class.

"He had darker hair and a big, bushy mustache," da Silva recalls, warming up to the challenge of describing her teacher thirty years ago. "He was cocky, and he was strict. Once, he taped our hands to keep the fingers from opening, and he expected me, at fourteen, to be able to

Kumu Patrick

ooh and ahh during a hula maʻi. He even stormed out of class once and turned over a table on his way out."

In 1991, Kumu Patrick moved to an airy Victorian flat on Potrero Hill, where he lived with his new partner, Buck Schmitz, a hairstylist in the neighborhood. It was during what he calls the Buck Years that he discovered the club scene. "I loved dancing, and I loved electronic music," he says simply, modestly admitting that he "did a little DJ-ing."

The original dancers of what was then called Nā Lei Hulu o Ka'ahumanu, circa 1985

A friend who was a club promoter invited Kumu Patrick to bring some dancers to a weekly party in the old Dreamland space, at Third and Harrison. "That was one of the most special performances of my life," Kumu Patrick says. "When I was young in Honolulu, we'd go out after a show to Hula's." (Hula's Bar and Lei Stand was a fixture, in the 1970s and '80s, for gays, tourists, and regular night owls.) "Here in San Francisco, though, the clubs were just my private life," he continues. "That night at Third and Harrison, it dawned on me: 'This is awesome and fucking weird. My worlds are colliding. Do I want to do this?'"

Some of the boundaries he'd carefully erected started to dissolve. Soon his dancers were performing in other clubs in California and beyond. Then he set a hula for Kamehameha and Ka'ahumanu to Terence Trent D'Arby. Then he choreographed "Salva Mea." His new style of "awesome and fucking weird" hula was emerging.

Eventually he had scores of students, including Hawaiians, Samoans, Chinese, Japanese, Filipinos, Latinos, *haole* (whites), Koreans, blacks, and many mixed-race mainlanders. Some were born and raised in Hawai'i. Some were born of Hawaiian parents but raised in the Bay Area. Some had no Hawai'i connections, but were nuts about ethnic dance.

He skimmed the seven best students—beautiful, young Hawaiian women—to put together a dance company in 1985 and named it Nā Lei Hulu o Kaʻahumanu, which means "The Feathered Wreaths of Queen Kaʻahumanu." (The queen is known as the most powerful of the twenty or more wives of Kamehameha the Great.) "I decided on that name in homage to the queen's appreciation for beauty—and in a nod to her acuity. She included the loveliest girls from around the islands in her retinue, but she knew it was *kapu*, or forbidden, for Kamehameha to take any member of her court as a wife or lover. She was nobody's fool."

Kumu Patrick then set about choreographing for festivals and fundraisers, special events and spectacular parties. "We once went to New Orleans for Halloween, for a weekend of festivities benefiting an AIDS hospice," Kumu Patrick remembers. "We are dancing for eight thousand people at a dance party, and everyone *stops* what they're doing, enthralled. And the next day, at the House of Blues, they ask us to do some hula—we're on after the Gospel Singers—and we do 'Kaʻena.' The applause is so loud that Pam, one of the dancers, starts crying. And then the audience starts crying, and then we *all* start crying." Kumu Patrick's voice goes from pumped to pensive. "The night before was an extravaganza, but this is just simple, homegrown hula. Here we are, dancing regular 'auana, and these people are going absolutely nuts."

Nā Lei Hulu became a mainstay at the San Francisco Ethnic Dance Festival and performed throughout California, as well as in Honolulu, Reno, Las Vegas, New Orleans, New York City, and Washington, DC. Kumu Patrick and his hālau were also profiled in the 2003 PBS documentary film *American Aloha: Hula Beyond Hawaiʻi*.

But by then the name of the company had changed. Kumu Patrick had gotten a call from his kumu, whose full name is Robert Uluwehionāpuaikawēkiuokalani Cazimero. The student of Maiki had named his hālau (Nā Kamalei o Līlīlehua) in part after *his* kumu, who was known as Līlīlehua. He suggested Kumu Patrick follow the same pattern, replacing "o Kaʻahumanu" with "i ka Wēkiu"—part of his own middle name.

"I was taken aback," Kumu Patrick says. "Giving someone your Hawaiian name binds you to them indefinitely and, in effect, offers approval and validation. I offered Kumu my gratitude, hung up the phone, then left it off the hook in case he called me back to change his mind."

He didn't, of course. Kumu Patrick notes another dimension to his evolving connection with Cazimero. "The tether to our *piko* [umbilical cord] in Hawaiʻi was strengthened. We were now Nā Lei Hulu i ka Wēkiu, which means "The Many Feathered Wreaths, at the Summit, Held in High Esteem."

Kumu Patrick has been building an impressive hālau ever since. Today, Nā Lei Hulu comprises a professional company of forty dancers, as well as eight weekly classes for some three hundred adults and children. Students start when they are as young as four, and there is no upward age limit. They range from rank beginners to those who have been studying for decades.

San Francisco turns out to have been very good for Kumu Patrick, despite the fact that at first the hula scene in the city was anything but robust. "In the '80s, California had the reputation of being the ugly stepsister or the mangy mutt of hula," he muses. "There's still a perception that we're not on a par with groups from Hawaiʻi." Yet San Francisco's freewheeling spirit, and its distance from Hawaiʻi, worked to his advantage. "Twenty years ago, someone said to me, 'It must be so nice that you're teaching hula in San Francisco without anybody looking over your shoulder.' There's great freedom in that."

He's used that freedom to do his own thing. Early on, he decided to forgo hula competitions, which is how most kumu hula get their hālau onto the big stage. He took his company into underground dance festivals and he tapped into mainland showcases like the Smithsonian National Museum of the American Indian. The ethnomusicologist Amy K. Stillman notes that other island performers were also exploring alternate

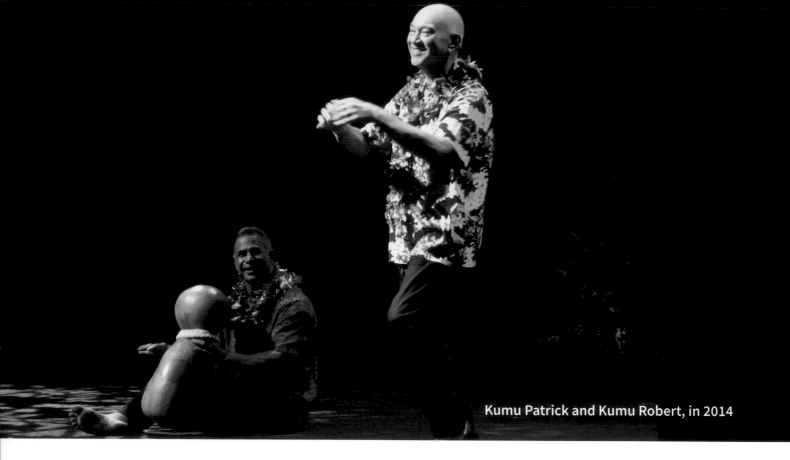

venues for hula. The Hawai'i Island school Hālau o Kekuhi, for example, had performed a hula opera, *Holo Mai Pele*, for PBS, and, of course, Cazimero's Nā Kamalei had performed at the Royal Hawaiian's Monarch Room, as well as at Carnegie Hall in 1989 and the Miss America pageant in 1992. (The Brothers Cazimero also always included dancing by the kumu hula Leina'ala Heine at their annual performances at the Hawai'i Theatre and the Waikīkī Shell.)

"Patrick has been one of the most articulate kumu hula about explicitly moving away from competition and pursuing other possibilities of stagecraft," notes Stillman. "And he found his way into financial circuits to make that possible."

"We're supported by the city, by the state, and by wonderful organizations like the Alliance for California Traditional Arts," says Kumu Patrick. Grants have come from the San Francisco Arts Commission, the Zellerbach Family Foundation, and the Honolulu-based Alexander & Baldwin Foundation. "While I was learning how to get grants, my hula brethren back home were holding car washes. They still struggle to get the financial support they deserve."

Awards have come as well, among them recognition in 1998 for outstanding work in the Asian-Pacific community in San Francisco, a "lifetime achievement" from the San Francisco Ethnic Dance Festival in 2006, and choreographer commissions from both the Wallace Alexander Gerbode Foundation and the William and Flora Hewlett Foundation in 2012.

Those who know him personally, of course, view Kumu Patrick as more than a collection of bullet points on a CV. His former partner and longtime friend Bob Davis calls Kumu Patrick "self-realized." UH-Mānoa professor Puakea Nogelmeier, a frequent collaborator, notes, "Patrick's pleasant, he has charisma, he lacks

The Monday-night sophomore class

"Salva Mea (Radio Edit)"

arrogance—he would do fine as a car salesman, a manager, or whatever other occupation he would go into." But, Nogelmeier adds, "he has an intensity of purpose. And he is a lot smarter than he lets on. He's both sophisticated and exposed—he's worldly."

BACK TO THE SOURCE

Worldly or not, Kumu Patrick felt something was missing in his albeit rich mainland experience. And so, in 2000, after receiving an Irvine Fellowship in dance, he decided to go back to his roots. For the next three years, Kumu Patrick traveled to Oʻahu once a month to participate in ʻūniki training with one of Aunti Maiki's protégées, Mae Kamāmalu Klein, to whom Aunti Maiki had entrusted her repertoire and her ʻūniki ritual. The rigorous training Kumu Patrick put himself through involved meticulously researching every chant, which, in turn, meant learning vocabulary; breaking down kaona (metaphors, double entendres, and purposely veiled meanings); reviewing pertinent myths and legends; and casting about for all necessary historical summaries, references, and anecdotes—not to mention developing personal thoughts and summations for each chant, song, or dance.

"Aunti is slight and spry," Kumu Patrick says about his third kumu. "But her physical attributes belie her stature in hula. She represents complete authority and immense knowledge."

'ŪNIKI

From 2000 to 2003, Kumu Patrick underwent 'ūniki training with Aunti Mae Kamāmalu Klein, graduating as a kumu hula. Aunti Mae herself was a part of Aunti Maiki's legendary 1973 Papa 'Ūniki class, and she inherited her kumu's 'ūniki mantle the old-fashioned way: she walked with Aunti Maiki through every 'ūniki performed from 1973 to 1983.

The end of the period of 'ūniki training culminates in a two-day event that honors deities and chiefs, celebrates the lineage of the hālau, and follows strict protocol dictating everything from what students wear to how they prepare the food to which parts of the pig they're allowed to eat. Much of the 'ūniki proceedings are kept guarded, if not secret, though aspects of it have been reported over time.

In Aunti Maiki's tradition, a prominent feature of the event is that the new teachers are put through a series of rituals and tests. Candidates are expected to dance, chant, and display the superior knowledge of the initiated throughout both days of the 'ūniki. Each step of the process is closely scrutinized, and students learn who will graduate at which level only very early on the final day. Other distinguished kumu hula and *kupuna* (elders in the community) come to help, witness, and judge whether a dancer is ready to receive the title of *'ōlapa* (dancer), *ho'opa'a* (chanter), or *kumu hula* (teacher).

On the second day, families and friends of the graduates are invited to a Hawaiian feast, or *lū'au*, and to observe their first performances as 'ōlapa, ho'opa'a, and kumu.

Classes became increasingly formal, as dancers were required to wear traditional adornments and were accompanied by rarely perfomed dressing chants. "I felt as if I were a priest in church, but a church that resonated with me," Kumu Patrick says. "In this one, I could really feel a connection to a higher power."

Some of the instruction involved fashioning his own instruments, such as the *pahu* (drum), *ipu heke* (double gourd), *'ulī'ulī* (feathered gourd rattler), and *pūniu* (small knee drum). "Constructing the pahu took several months," Kumu Patrick remembers. "It started with finding a log from a coconut tree, then removing the hard, dried, thick skin and digging out the center. I had to create a design to carve on the drum, then carve it. In all this, we had to adhere to a strict use of manual tools. There was a lot of pounding, huffing, and puffing. After the first day, my body was sore for a week. I slept every night dreaming of power tools."

The relationship with a kumu is like a *pīkake* (jasmine) blossom that begins as a tightly closed bud and opens slowly over time to reveal its fragrant essence. "Aunti Mae is loving and kind and all of that, but she's not a pushover," says Kumu Patrick about his kumu. "She can be exacting and finicky." She can also provide her charges with moments of unexpected mirth. One of Kumu Patrick's favorite stories about Aunti Mae—pulled out often when he is teaching an *oli kāhea*, or chant asking permission to enter a class to receive instruction— conveys this side of her.

"During the first months of studying with Aunti," he usually begins, "I was with two others outside of the hālau, waiting for the designated time to begin our oli kāhea, asking her to open the door and welcome us in. We had only chanted it once before. We started pleadingly, with great fervor. No response from the other side of the closed door. Aunti hadn't told us what to do if we asked, and she didn't answer." (The kumu typically answer with an *oli komo*, a welcoming chant granting permission to enter the place of instruction.)

"This had to be a test," he continues. "We decided that she wanted us to use another oli kāhea, which we rendered very lovingly. Still no response. We had one more to try, the most difficult of the batch. We took deep breaths and chanted with great affection and presence. Our execution was sublime. I was sure the doors were going to burst open on their own. We waited. No response. By now, we felt like complete failures—lost and confused. We scoured our notes to see what vital piece we neglected. All of a sudden, a blue streak of steel sped down the driveway, jerking unceremoniously to a stop in the garage. Out from the sedan pops Aunti Mae. 'Did you get my message that I was running late?' she asked. 'I hope you guys were practicing!'"

In 2003, Kumu Patrick was formally ordained as a kumu hula at Kahiauakamalanai, an estate on Oʻahu's windward side. With this official designation comes an attendant obligation to perpetuate the wisdom of those who came before him. Kumu Patrick has since instituted his own ʻūniki process of traditional studies and found ways to immerse his senior dancers in hula tradition.

His becoming a formal kumu hula changed his teaching, and even his choreography. If Robert Cazimero gave him bombast, Aunti Mae softened it. If Cazimero brought out his inner showman, Aunti Mae brought out his inner pedagogue. Kumu Patrick regularly pauses a dance class, brings out the cafeteria tables, and strings Hawaiian words like so many kukui nuts across a whiteboard, explaining chants from the inside out.

"He's so free," Aunti Mae says about her student. We are sitting at Zippy's on Vineyard Boulevard in Honolulu. Aunti Mae—as slight as a reed, with neatly cut short hair and thinly plucked eyebrows—has arrived in dark pants and a magenta blouse with a tucked front. Her eyeglasses hang on a cord around her long neck. (She later tells me that the reason she always wears pants is that they're what Aunti Maiki wore.)

She talks about her life in hula and her San Francisco student. "He has the ability to walk in two worlds," she says. "But when he's gonna go Hawaiian, he goes all the way. Whenever he does that kahiko side, he is *us* and he wears that blue."

"That blue" is the light, almost ice-blue color Aunti Maiki chose for the *kīhei* of her graduates. The kīhei is a long, one-shoulder garment printed with the symbols of a particular hula line, and it is one of the signs of the authority of a person who has gone through the ʻūniki process.

"I'm just pleased that he has taken what I taught him and he teaches that to his students," Aunti Mae continues.

Aunti Mae is also very fond of Kumu Patrick's innovative hula, and she doesn't see it as a breach of protocol, or a break from hālau tradition. "Maiki had a very creative side," she says. "She did pageants. She did the *Aloha ʻOe* story, using all of her students—complete with a horse onstage! Though she always asked her elders for permission."

Does she have a favorite among his signature pieces? "'First Time,'" she says, naming the flowing hula danced to Roberta Flack's "The First Time Ever I Saw Your Face." The women wear long, black velvet dresses and two extravagant white lily blossoms tucked into chignons. "He found a way to put the emotions into that dance."

Papa ʻŪniki Lehua, 2006

"A ka Lunā o Pu'u Onioni"

THE NĀ LEI HULU MOVES

What, specifically, marks the style of a Nā Lei Hulu dancer? Kumu Patrick jumps up from his kitchen table and stands barefoot on the hardwood floor. "A lot of the motions we use are Robert's," he says, demonstrating the Robert Cazimero style. "It's in the way we move our hips—we roll them through the movement of the feet." He is doing a kāholo, and it moves like a bolt of energy through the lower body: the knee bends, the foot lifts, the hip lifts, the foot steps, the hip lowers—and then the hip keeps rolling as the sequence begins with the other foot.

He calls particular attention to the extension of his entire body. "In the old style," he says, "the knees and the elbows are bent." His muscled limbs retract to illustrate. His hands, held close, move mildly. "Aunti Maiki was one of the first to stand up, to dance in *i luna*," he continues, his entire body lifting inexorably, his spine lengthening like a yoga teacher's, his limbs extending. "Hula became elegant, but gently so. She also standard-ized movements and emphasized technique, so that the dancers became more unified."

Kumu Patrick also credits Robert Cazimero with the more vigorous elements of his dance. By now he is moving back and forth, parallel to the kitchen cabinets, his arms reach-ing out to an imaginary audience. "With Robert there is a power, a statuesque quality."

The muscled arms reach out, but there is tension, as though an invisible filament is pulling the fingers outward and the elbow backward. There is an aliveness in every fiber. "Robert took Aunti Maiki's hula vocabulary and increased it. His men embodied an athletic grace.

"I'm always working on increasing that vocabulary."

Hula Guyz with Hālau nā Kamalei o Līlīlehua

Kumu Hula Francine Aarona, Mae Klein, Kalei Aarona-Lorenzo

The particular way that Kumu Patrick has found to stir emotions is a common theme when his teachers (not to mention dance critics) reflect upon his particular contribution to hula. When Cazimero is asked what makes his student distinct, he answers without a pause: "The whole hula mua thing," referring to the mysterious fusion of music, staging, lights, and storytelling in Nā Lei Hulu productions. "It can stir different emotions, even sadness and anger. It's great theater."

But even if such innovations take his hula far from the World War II–era living room of Lōkālia Montgomery, Kumu Patrick still feels firmly bound to his hula line. "We do perform a few dances that came to us from Lōkālia," he notes, "and even more that come from Aunti Maiki." He says that Aunti Maiki is ever present in other ways, too. "I see her when I see Kumu Robert in certain moments—like when he is wearing a *lei poʻo*, a garland on his head, and he tilts his head with a certain smile. I also see her in all the ways that Aunti Mae is nurturing, confident, respectful, and loving."

It's a lineage defined by strong emotional ties. "In the way Aunti Mae talks about Aunti Maiki, the way she loves her—that's the way I feel about Aunti Mae. She has given me an anchor, so that when I'm playing on the edge, I don't fall off."

"Lei Kapa 'Ehu Kai Ka'ena na ka Makani"

PART II

Mo'olelo ("Stories")

The Natives Are Restless premièred in 1996 and marked the first time Kumu Patrick Makuakāne tried out a new style of hula on a wide audience. In it, he paired mostly traditional hula movements with very untraditional costuming, staging, and music, including electronic remixes. He also went narrative, interpreting history over a suite of dances, rather than in single "numbers." Natives evolved with successive productions, and for the show's twentieth anniversary in 2016, Kumu Patrick added a second act. In the meantime, he continued to explore ways in which hula could tell the stories that he, as a modern Hawaiian, wanted to tell. He began to mix hula kahiko, hula 'auana, and his new style, which gained the moniker hula mua, or "progressive hula."

He also began to take on new themes, expressing them in narrative works of varying lengths. Daughters of Haumea (2006) looks at the role of women in ancient Hawai'i; Māui: Turning Back the Sky (2008) portrays the Polynesian hero Māui and the ancient art of navigation; The Kumulipo (2010) takes a Hawaiian creation chant as inspiration; Mele Kapalakiko (2011) explores the links between San Francisco and Hawai'i; and Ka Leo Kānaka (2013) finds inspiration in a century of Hawaiian-language newspapers. The three full-scale narrative productions here are arranged in rough chronology—not in terms of theatrical début, but in terms of the grand sweep of Hawaiian history.

"Akua Mo'o"

CHAPTER FOUR

Daughters of Haumea

Ask your average audience member to describe a man from ancient Hawai'i, and you might get all kinds of answers, from the shark god to the pig rascal, from fearsome warriors to flawless fishermen, from the god Kāne to Kamehameha the Great. Ask the same person to point to a woman, however, and you are likely to get one consistent response: Pele. The tempestuous goddess of the volcano has so imprinted herself on our collective imagination that you'd almost think she was the Hawaiian Eve.

But Pele is only one of many heroines of ancient Hawai'i, and *Daughters of Haumea,* which débuted in 2006, puts the spotlight (or the colored gels) on several who have been long overlooked. In fact, looming over the show—figuratively and literally—is the real Hawaiian Eve: Pele's mother, the goddess Haumea, or "She Who Gives Birth." Onstage in the Nā Lei Hulu i ka Wēkiu production, she is represented by a statue almost as tall as Burning Man, perched on two stout, arching legs, draped in fabric, and bathed in lights that shift from forest green to lava red.

Daughter Natalie Mahina Jensen, left, and mother Lucia Tarallo Jensen visit hula practice at Daniel Webster Elementary School.

For the show's introductory remarks, Kumu Patrick walks barefoot onstage and launches into the background story, telling his audience that he drew inspiration from a book of the same name by scholar Lucia Tarallo Jensen and her daughter, Natalie Mahina Jensen.

Lucia Tarrallo Jensen's newest effort followed another, written with her husband, Rocky Ka'ioliokahi-hikolo'ehu Jensen, whom Kumu Patrick describes as "a Hawaiian artist extraordinaire—a sculptor, illustrator, designer, builder." That book, *Ka Po'e Kāne Kahiko*, or *The Men of Ancient Hawai'i*, is about the various roles of men in traditional times, with each archetype depicted in a graphite illustration by Rocky. "The combination of the illustrations and the text, describing our history from a native perspective," Kumu Patrick says, "gave me a powerful sense of pride about my heritage."

But in researching the book about ancient men, Lucia became aware how much Hawaiian history was written from a male point of view. More important, she noticed, most of the men writing that history were either strangers to Hawaiian culture or Christian converts whose perspective was skewed by religious beliefs. The biases only got worse when it came to their depictions of women. So she decided to write a companion book to set the record straight.

"Haumea is Mother Earth, giving life to virtually all things," Kumu Patrick tells his audience. "Hawaiians believed that everything flows from within the female awareness—the gift of life, death and rebirth, all organic activity. These have no parallel male awareness. Because of this divine authority, woman has always held an elevated and honored place in Polynesian society.

"We now recognize that Hawaiian women were an integral part of the Hawaiian identity—the female principle was clearly woven into civilization's fabric; it was essential to all facets of life. Woman was the divine companion, the equalizer, the balance in all male-oriented rituals.

"Whew!" He exhales. "What a mouthful. I feel like the Hawaiian Gloria Steinem."

The crowd laughs, and he warms to the spirit.

"Over twenty years ago, I started this hālau with seven women. They have been the motivating factor in everything I do with hula. Their grace, beauty, intelligence, and complexity have been a continual inspiration since day one. It's a good thing I'm gay, because I would have fallen in love with many of them. How messy and inappropriate that would have been! Now, instead of wanting to get them out of a dress, all I want to do is put them in one."

The crowd laughs again, and the show begins.

THE SACRED AND WONDROUS MOTHER

The first dance starts with a literal bang—in this case, with a peal of thunder and the roar of an ancient chant that seems to come from Kumu Patrick's deepest place:

> *E Haumea hoʻāno akua*
> *E Haumea hoʻāno makuahine āiwaiwa . . .*
> *E Haumea o nā kino pāpālehu*
> *i manomano i ka lehulehu o nā kino*
> *ʻO Haumeanui hoʻāiwaiwa!*

The curtain is still drawn, and onto the black fabric the chant's translation is projected in English as he chants:

> Oh, Haumea, sacred akua
> Oh, Haumea, sacred and wondrous mother . . .
> Oh, Haumea of the four hundred thousand bodies
> four thousand fold are her many forms
> Oh, Great Haumea, causing wonder!

"'O Hina Ho'i"

HAWAIIAN CHANT

Daughters of Haumea relies upon a number of different kinds of chants, or mele. In ancient Hawai'i, culture and religion were inextricably bound, so prayers to the gods were always chanted. The kapu (sacredness) and mana (power) of the chant were encoded in its text.

The profundity of the text is carried in the kaona, often translated as "hidden meaning." Chants are composed with layers of meanings, so the kaona might be expressed through metaphor. And the metaphor might have more than one hidden meaning. A particular flower, for example, like the pua līlīlehua, or red sagebrush flower, might be recognized as a symbol for a person (like Aunti Maiki Aiu Lake) but might carry other associations as well (the wind and rain in Pālolo Valley, or the maiden who lived in the valley and was courted by a mythical lizard). Further, private associations might be known only to the author of a chant.

Chanters of old had to be well versed in the language, myths, history, and rules of poetic imagery. Training was formal and vigorous. A chanter was expected to accurately, and in one sitting, memorize chants that were scores—or even hundreds—of lines long. They often had to grasp the entire composition after hearing it a single time. Any musical stress on a word, made consciously or unconsciously, could change meaning. Facial expression, eyes, and even eyebrow movement might communicate as much as a word.

Chant types include *kānaenae* (praise), *pule* or *kau* (prayer), *kū'auhau* or *ko'ihonua* (genealogy), *kanikau* or *kūmākena* (wail or lament), *pana* or *'āina* (place), and *hakuole* (derision or mockery).

Some of the more common chant types refer in some way to a named individual:

Mele inoa: a name chant
Mele ma'i: a chant in praise of a particular person's procreative power
Mele lei: a chant presented to an individual, together with a lei
Mele ho'āla: an individual's awakening chant
Mele he'e nalu: an individual's surfing chant

Some chants are used for games, amusement, or playful improvisation. The most popular chant type today is the love chant (*mele ho'oipoipo*), characterized by elegant language and figurative references to the loved one. Many love chants have been adapted to contemporary Hawaiian tunes, as have chants extolling important or familiar places (mele 'āina).

Mele inoa honoring Luahine Lea

Training included projection, elocution, enunciation, and vocal techniques, but once a chanter was trained and did not distort the words beyond recognition, he or she had a certain latitude. Final vowels or entire syllables might be whispered, dropped completely, or lengthened if the beat seemed to demand it. The chanter might, at will, replace *k* with *t* or, occasionally, with *s*. Personal expression was and is a plus, especially if it entices an audience to listen more intently.

The imitation of natural sounds—different birds, wind, water dripping or rushing—was a favorite training method. One historian refers to developing control for increasing and diminishing tone by imitating the breaking and receding of incoming waves. One twentieth-century chanter is said to have used his wife's vacuum cleaner for the same purpose.

"Calling All Angels"

The chanting continues, and the curtain opens. Men and women pour out from the loins of the giant statue onstage. Maybe not four hundred thousand of them, but you get the idea. They creep forward to the hypnotizing beat, sweeping their arms before them, men in sarongs and women in skirts with bustles on each hip that set off their every movement.

A series of dances traces the births of the various ancestral gods, starting with Haumea herself and proceeding through her daughters Hina (the beautiful goddess of the moon), Pele (goddess of the volcano, born as a flame in Haumea's mouth), and Kapo (the shape-shifting goddess of fertility, sorcery, and hula).

The women in the troupe still outnumber the men, but even in this suite about Haumea's daughters, Kumu Patrick varies the tone by letting the men get into the act, in a number honoring Pele's brother, the shark god Kamohoali'i.

The tone shifts again, dramatically, in the last dance of the suite. The song "Calling All Angels," by Jane Siberry, starts to play, and women return to the stage, simply dressed, without either voluminous skirts or strands of lei. The lights darken to deep blue, and a lone woman's voice chants to Haumea, her words switching from Hawaiian to English, then settling in English:

E ala ē!
Awaken!
E ala ē!
Awaken!
Awaken!
Awaken, ancestral women, guardians from the spirit world
Awaken, all forty thousand
Awaken, ancestral goddesses in the heavens
Awaken, beloved women dwelling in the spirit world
Enter and inspire us
Awaken!
Awaken!
The words have flown!

The beat of the drum is gone, as is the rumbling of Kumu Patrick's chanting. Fragments of language (the names of Catholic saints) in Siberry's song fade, then are overlaid, then replaced, by an electronic mix of guitar strings, bells, cellos, and a lone soprano. The lights brighten. The costumes shimmer: soft pink, plum, silver. The music is lyrical, sweet, even a touch melancholic.

This is classic Kumu Patrick: a sudden changeup in which he throws a new element into the mix. Here, it's mostly a matter of setting traditional hula movements to very untraditional music. "The song is so beautiful, it kills me," he says later in an interview, giving the how and why of ending a suite of dances about ancient Hawaiian goddesses with a pop song. "I first heard it on an episode of *Six Feet Under*. Several women were gathered in the basement of a funeral home, surrounding the body of a recently departed friend. They sang this song, holding hands, while the body was embalmed and dressed for the funeral."

The painfully melodic lyrics describe "trying, hoping, hurting, loving, crying" and implore the angels to "walk me through this one, don't leave me alone."

"I Am Stretched on Your Grave"

"This song says it all: life can be a shit show some-times, and you gotta call the angels. Of course, the angels *we* are calling are Hina, Pele, and Kapo," Kumu Patrick says. "We are asking these female entities for help."

But there are other layers of meaning. The singer herself is calling *her* angels: Santa Maria, Santa Teresa, Santa Anna, Santa Susannah, Santa Cecilia, and Santa Copelia, among others. "In my mind," Kumu Patrick continues, "the Italian and Latin names link the song to Lucia. So that's my own bit of kaona, my own secret meaning. I am calling out to Lucia and acknowledging all she has done to help me."

"My grandmother, mother, sister, and aunt took the reins of my childhood," Kumu Patrick continues. "I was spoiled and scolded—but mostly showered with love. My father, a kind and loving man, was around but not actively engaged in raising me. That made it difficult for me to feel close to him. But with my mom there, I always felt safe and adored. That's another kaona—*Daughters* is my tribute to them."

Kumu Patrick's grandma Alyce Kuʻualoha

THE ANCESTRAL ANGELS

From the most primordial Hawaiian goddesses—and the European saints—the story shifts to the ancestral goddesses, lesser but still legendary women who made Hawaiian society tick: the oracles and fisherwomen and healers and courtesans. These are women whose roles Jensen discovered and fleshed out through her scholarship. Some of them are literal, some not. Some of these figures are spirits and totems who guide the actions of men and women. Some are classes of common women with critical roles in ancient Hawaiʻi. They include:

- *Nā Hoʻokele* (**Those Who Prepare the Dead for Burial**). Devoted relatives and retainers who willingly underwent a period of defilement in order to follow all the rituals of burial of their loved ones. These included scraping the flesh from the bones, apportioning the relics among family and friends, and chanting dirges that lamented the death while recounting the life of the deceased.

- *Ka Lawaiʻa Kōkō* (**The Women's Fishing Guild**). If the open sea belonged in the realm of man, the shoreline, reef, rivers, and fishponds for kelp and shrimp belonged in the realm of women. On moonlit nights, the women of the fishing guild would hitch up their skirts, walk along the shore, and feel with their fingertips for rock squid, young demoiselle, and *hou*, or "snoring" fish.

HAUMEA'S DAUGHTERS

Polynesian voyagers crisscrossed the Pacific, settling the Hawaiian archipelago last, after Fiji, Easter Island, New Zealand, Samoa, the Cook Islands, Tonga, and Tahiti. Various islanders share myths and legends, but the stories of Haumea and her daughters have taken particular twists and turns in the Hawaiian Islands.

Pele. Volcano goddess was born as a flame in the mouth of Haumea. Countless stories attribute rock and landforms to Pele's wrath. Before settling at Kīlauea, she dug craters now extinct—Diamond Head, Koko Crater, Salt Lake, and so on. She appeared at different times as fire, a wrinkled hag, a child, and a beautiful girl.

Hiʻiaka-i-ka-poli-o-Pele (literally, "Hiʻiaka in the bosom of Pele"). Pele's favorite younger sister was born from the mouth of Haumea, rather than from the bosom, as were the many other Hiʻiaka sisters. Born as an egg, she was carried under Pele's bosom until she became a young beauty. She transformed many evil *moʻo* into stones that are still visible. One of her forms was the *palaʻā* (lace fern, used to treat diseases, and one of the first plants to grow on new lava). As the physician of the Pele family, she resuscitated Chief Lohiʻau, the object of Pele's obsession. She also instituted the eating of fish from head to tail. Hula dancers worshiped her.

Kapo. One of Haumea's many children, and sister to Pele and Hiʻiaka, Kapo is associated with fertility and sorcery and is most famous for having detachable genitalia. Kapo is closely linked to Laka and is honored at the kuahu ("altar"). The goddesses are said to share a spirit—in some stories, Kapo is Laka's mother, while in others, they are the same goddess.

- *Hale o Papa* (**The Keepers of the Shrine of Papa**). Although men—in their role as guards of the celestial—presided over sacred temples, women were the guiding forces at the Hale ʻo Papa, the small chapel devoted to Mother Earth within the state temple complex, where images of female ancestors were kept. Women also guided men through a metaphysical rebirth after important ceremonial functions.

- *Luahine Lea* (**The Patroness of Canoe Makers**). Man built canoes, but he relied on the *ʻelepaio* bird to tell him which trees were sound. The ʻelepaio is a totem of Lea, the patroness of canoe builders, so without her participation no canoe could be launched.

"Hoe Puna"

- *He Wāhine Mākaukau no ke Kaunu* (**Women Skilled in the Art of Lovemaking**). To be sexually adept and sensually alive—and to have the ability to experience unrestrained desire—was as important to ancient Hawaiians as having sex to produce offspring. The vital energy caused by desire and passion was itself worshiped and idolized. The art of lovemaking belonged to the female realm, and both male and female adolescents were carefully coached in foreplay, pleasurable positions, the making of aphrodisiacs, and birth control. Their aunties and elders, wāhine mākaukau no ke kāunu, were their teachers.

- *Makāula* (**The Oracle**). Possessing "eyes to the spirit world," the seers of ancient Hawai'i were said to have a psychic rapport and could cross the mystical threshold to communicate with powers dwelling in other realms. Their rare talent of *'ike pāpālua* ("second sight") allowed them to communicate with guardian spirits and foretell events. The makāula could call ancestors to come as a wind and hover over the head of the seer. Methods of concentration employed flames, piles of pebbles, *'awa* (kava shrubs), and the reflection made by placing a highly polished obsidian mirror in a calabash filled with water.

- *Ka Po'ohulu* (**The Masters of Featherwork**). Featherworking was primarily a women's discipline. The *kāhili*, or cylindrical feather staff, is an object whose shape echoes the spiraling *ti*

Makāula (The Oracle)

plant; among its various uses, it acted as a soul-catcher in funeral processions. Also included in this discipline were the many varied feather garlands, including *lei hulu* (feather lei), that allowed women to momentarily join their avian companions.

- *Akua Moʻo* (**Dragon Totem**). The akua moʻo is to fresh waterways as Pele is to the volcanoes. The "dragon goddess" was considered a source of great sanctity and, through the families entrusted with the kuleana ("responsibility") for the river, assured the astute management of water resources. A properly nurtured akua moʻo would respond with plentiful water for taro and crops; a neglected akua moʻo would unleash her fury in the form of floods.

Each of these archetypes gets a dance in the show. Some dances are in the "ancient" style of kahiko, some in the "modern" style of ʻauana, some in the "postmodern" style of hula mua. The "Featherwork" number features a nineteenth-century seated hula and elaborate feather staffs. The "Akua Moʻo" features a former Paul Taylor dancer, Rachel Berman, who slithers around with a lizard spine and tail.

Women dominate most of the dances, but the men do get one, a fantastic bird dance: "Manu ʻŌʻō." The mele mentions the work of the *kia manu*, or ancient bird-catchers, who placed gummy sap on branches to trap unsuspecting birds, which were set free after their most colorful feathers were plucked. One part of the hula

"Akua Moʻo"

"PROGRESSIVE" HULA

Those who dance hula hear the phrase *i mua* with some frequency. It's a teacher's way of delivering a stage direction, gently beckoning dancers to move forward in their dance rows. But the term *hula mua* didn't exist until a few years after Kumu Patrick invented the form, which initially stemmed from his desire to combine hula movements with his favorite non-Hawaiian music, whether opera, pop, or electronic music.

The word *mua* can refer to either the past or the future, as is evident in phrases like *ma mua aku nei* ("some time ago"), *keia mua a'e* ("the distant future"), and *holo i mua* ("to progress"). For Kumu Patrick, *hula mua* refers to dance that "takes from the past and brings to the future."

One of Kumu Patrick's secondary goals with hula mua was to reestablish the once-essential audience role in hula. In the early days, he argues, audiences were more easily involved in the performance because they understood the language and the word plays and poetic layers Hawaiian composers are fond of. But since most viewers today don't have language as an entry point, he needed to find other ways to engage them. That's why he relies on so much contemporary, non-Hawaiian music, including remixes.

He's particularly drawn to songs with lyrics that echo sentiments found in Hawaiian poetry. For example, one line of Madonna's "Rain" ("Your love's coming down on me like rain") seemed so reminiscent of Hawaiian poetry that he felt his choreography could restore for present-day audiences hula's traditional link between movements and words.

Hula mua also gives Kumu Patrick the freedom to bust stereotypes and let hula express a broader spectrum of emotions than the typical joyous or sensuous dances do. He draws inspiration from sources in the Hawaiian tradition that are "raw and turbulent," he says, like creation chants and kanikau. An example of the latter is "I Am Stretched on Your Grave," set to a traditional Irish poem rendered in contemporary song. In the dance, women wail over a corpse while others dance somberly in the background, interrupting their lovely vamps to reach out to the body and then to beat their chests. The dance expresses the very essence of hula mua.

shows the birds with feet caught by the sticky substance; they try to fly away, wings flapping furiously. The frenetic beating of the men's arms captures the birds' frenzied attempts to escape. The highly prized feathers that the bird-catchers attained would be crafted into feather cloaks and helmets for male high chiefs—stunning symbols of their high rank and heavenly power. "There is a proverb that mentions 'heated rain,'" says Kumu Patrick. "Warriors and chiefs in feather capes and helmets looked like little rainbows, or rain 'heated' by the sun. 'Manu 'Ō'ō' is a heated hula."

"Hana Aloha"

Men—or one man—play a different sort of role in the "Women Skilled in the Art of Love" segment. "In all levels of society, unskilled lovemaking was considered socially unacceptable," Kumu Patrick, back onstage to introduce the dance, says coyly. "The Hawaiians understood the protocol of courting and mating as akin to 'ecstasy and joy.' We're talking *Kama Sutra*–level philosophy!

"Although man was a willing and aggressive participant in lovemaking, it was the woman who developed that primal urge into an art form."

Then, to percussive instrumentation that sounds like a cross between a Cuban guiro and an insect's back legs, women enter the stage and surround a high bamboo daybed covered with luscious sheets and pillows. One woman leads a young man, made to seem extra innocent by his black Dickies work shorts and white shirt, onto the love bed. The other women circle the couple, dancing an *'ōniu*, a hula step that allows the hips to move in sensuous figure eights. A young woman's voice echoes, speaking in Hawaiian. The two on the bed caress, reach, and gyrate their hips. The music drops into a deep house beat, and the two leave the bed and dance among the others. Other men join in, their gestures nothing short of graphic. Men and women couple, uncouple, go two-on-one. Disco never got this good. The dance is sizzling, tender, evocative, orgiastic.

The first couple returns to the bed and embraces. "A world so deep," intones an electronic voice. "So liquid. So deep, so deep, so liquid. So deep." The dancers collapse around the bier-bed in a pyramid of exhaustion.

"Kanikau"

TALKING STORY

Kumu Patrick returns to the stage as narrator every three or four dances, with running patter that fills in the audience on what they are seeing. Sometimes he relates myths, sometimes he cracks jokes, and sometimes he shares bits of his personal history, like when he was skeptical about some of his father's stories.

In Pidgin English, the patois of the islands, most stories begin with "You know small-kid time?" instead of "once upon a time." The first of Kumu Patrick's stories begins with shades of that patois, as he relates his father's claims about his family's guardian spirit.

"Ever since I was a small kid, my father told me that our family *'aumakua* was the shark. Once, he was spearfishing off the pier in Waimanalo, and he noticed all his friends were suddenly gone. Then he noticed a school of *manini*, or small green surgeonfish, passing. Then they were suddenly gone. Then he noticed a tiger shark, ten feet away. He's not moving, just floating in place, his tail moving back and forth. 'He jus' lookin' at me,' my dad said. 'I jus' lookin' right back at him. Then he go like this'"—Kumu Patrick jerks his head upward in the typical silent island greeting, a nonverbal "Howzit?" or "How's it going?"

The story continues with Kumu Patrick's father saying, "Then I go like this"—Kumu Patrick jerks his head again into the nonverbal obligatory response. Case closed: the spearfisherman and the tiger shark are brothers.

"I thought that was pretty cool," Kumu Patrick continues, his strong forearms gesticulating as he speaks. "Then I start to realize that *everybody's* 'aumakua is the shark. Ask *anyone* what their 'aumakua is—they always say the shark. Nobody says the hibiscus."

The audience laughs, and another suite of dances begins.

Later in the show, Kumu Patrick's most compelling monologue comes as he uses more family history to give context to the dance of nā hoʻokele, the funeral retainers of ancient Hawaiʻi. After an important person died, these kinswomen from the chiefly population removed decomposing flesh and organs from the departed. Then they scrubbed and scraped the long bones and the skull, wrapped the bones in *kapa*, or bark cloth, and finally went to the sea to bathe and purify themselves.

Afterward, dressed in black, with their jaws and chins blackened, they began a mourning vigil. Accompanied by the female elders of the deceased, the *hoʻokele* began the kanikau, or funeral chant, which commemorated the great beauty and noble deeds of the departed. The women wailed, swayed in unison, beat their chests with closed fists, and flailed their arms in despair. Their hypnotic dance continued for ten days. Their intense wailing let the soul know it should leave the physical body and enter the spirit world.

"I mean, this was a job that was not given to a stranger or some community mortician," Kumu Patrick comments, after explaining the tradition. "Only high-ranking chiefesses and retainers close to the departed were allowed to do this—mothers, daughters, sisters, aunts, grandmothers. How do you scrape off the flesh of your loved one to save the bones while retaining your spiritual integrity—and your sanity? You do it because . . . well, because it's necessary, and because you love a person that much."

WAIMANALO GOODBYE

The hoʻokele serve as special muses for Kumu Patrick, a fact that becomes clear when he launches into his next personal story, with his characteristic blend of irreverence and respect. "Before my mother passed away," he begins, "she would not tell us how she wanted to be buried. And she made it clear that she did not want us have a church burial for her.

"'What, Ma,' I asked, 'you want us put you in the backyard?'" He slips into Hawaiian creole. "She was adamant—no service. So when she did go, in 2002, we decided that she should be cremated and her ashes scattered at Waimanalo Beach, near the house.

"A few days before we were to scatter her ashes, my father says to me, 'So, you got the canoe?'

"'Canoe?' I asked back.

"'Yeah, the one you goin' take Mom out in.'

"'I don't know where to get a canoe,' I said. 'All my friends are hula dancers, not canoe paddlers. When they go beach, they no go in the water; they just stay on the sand and tan.'"

Kumu Patrick continues, "I suggested an alternative plan. I would put the urn with my mother's ashes in the crook of my arms like a football and swim out maybe fifty yards or so. (Not that I'd ever had a football in the crook of my arms, but I'd seen it on TV and it looked pretty easy.) I thought I'd get a nice distance away from the shore, open the urn underwater, let my mother out, have a moment, and swim back to shore.

"At that time, I was getting ready to have a hip replacement. I was somewhat crippled and a little heavy—not good if you're trying to imitate a running back.

"A very small group of family and close friends gathered on the beach. We said a few words and I headed into the ocean. It didn't take me long to realize that, uh-oh, this was way harder than I thought it was going to be.

"Like a dummy, I had scheduled the service right at high tide. This isn't Waikīkī Beach. This is Waimanalo.

"The swells were coming in rapidly enough to keep a fat, crippled person from looking like a hero. I'm barely fifteen feet from the shore, and I'm dying. (My advice to any of you planning to do this: get a canoe!)

William and Marie Makuakāne with Kumu Patrick's older sister, Patti

"I begin to realize there was no way I could paddle with one arm and hold Mom in the other. So I end up bouncing myself up from the sandy floor to get farther out while trying to take a breath each time I break through a crashing wave.

"Originally, I was planning on swimming out fifty yards, but I must have gotten fifty feet when I said, 'Ma, I gonna let you out here.' So I make one final bounce, take one last breath, submerge myself, open the urn, and make a swooping motion with my right arm, from left to right. Nothing. Swoop again. Nothing. I shake the urn. 'Ma, come out. Ma, I'm drowning.'

"My mother is not coming out.

"Then it dawns on me: I'm going to have to reach in and pull her out. So I begin scooping out her ashes. I'm jumping up, trying to get some air, and scooping out one batch after another. Before I know it, my mother's ashes are swirling all around me, through my hair, up my nose, in my mouth. For one brief second, I kinda freak out. Then I think, 'Wait a minute—this is the most sacred woman in the entire universe; no need panic. This is your mother. This is what you do when you love someone that much.'"

Kumu Patrick walks into the wings, and four women cross the stage, dragging a body laid out on a mat and weeping and wailing in what becomes a hard-to-listen-to lament. "*Auē*," they cry out, over and over. "Alas." They stop midstage and writhe above the inert body, howling as they do. A dozen graceful dancers in long black dresses and painted black jaws glide out and line up quietly behind them.

Kumu Patrick sings, a capella, a mournful English version of "I Am Stretched on Your Grave," the seventeenth-century Irish poem popularized by Sinéad O'Connor and Dead Can Dance. Ancient Hawai'i meets Gaelic tragedy.

Much of *Daughters of Haumea* has this esoteric, weighty, sometimes downright weird collision of dark subject matter, humorous personal story, and mesmerizing music and dance. It is often performed in the half-light, letting the audience privately grapple with topics not often talked about, much less danced about.

But Kumu Patrick always segues to lighter stuff, as when he follows "Nā Ho'okele" with a dance featuring the women of the fishing guild. They enter in calf-length dresses with circle skirts, shell lei on their heads and draping their necks. They also wear gracefully swaying kīhei, or sashes, made of real fishing nets, over one shoulder. The scrim turns to the watery colors of a gentle sea. The lilting voice of a female chanter accompanies their first dance, which is followed by a version of "Pūpū Hinuhinu," a lullaby about the cowrie shell, written in 1950 by Winona Beamer. The name of the song translates as "Shiny Shells" and is familiar to the children of Hawai'i; it reminds them to hold a cowrie to their ears so that the comforting waves can put them to sleep.

The last words of the show are left to Lucia Tarallo Jensen, in a voiceover, whose poetry remarks not just on the power of Haumea and her children, but on the power of stories themselves:

In the footsteps of our earth mother Haumea
We, her children, follow
Here is the prayer
It rises
It flies
The words have flown.

"'Au'a 'Ia"

CHAPTER FIVE

The Natives Are Restless

One day in 1995, Kumu Patrick was researching Hawaiian history when he stumbled upon the journals of missionaries who had arrived in Hawai'i in 1820. The missionary leader was Hiram Bingham, whose austere countenance and penchant for stiff white collars and black frock coats are captured later in daguerreotypes.

"I was curious about the thoughts of Bingham and his group when they were on the brig *Thaddeus* and seeing Hawai'i for the first time," Kumu Patrick says, reflecting on that moment. What he found shocked him. The missionaries' notes brimmed with contempt and quotes from the Bible. Where they might have described verdant shores or vibrant colors, they instead painted a picture of a "dark, ruined land" and people filled with unrighteousness, fornication, and wickedness. These people were not just "savages"—they were "whisperers, backbiters, haters of god, and inventors of evil things." The hula was a "devil's nest," designed only to promote lasciviousness.

"Here he was, coming to save us," the kumu hula says of Bingham and his cohort, "but we needed saving from *him*. I was incensed."

We are sitting in an office in San Francisco's South of Market district, where he has arrived with a bouquet of flowers and a sample of homemade bread pudding. His usual effusive demeanor disappears as he sits up in his chair, dark eyes blazing. "I started thinking about how many of us Hawaiians live under the muzzle of Christianity. We let another culture from thousands of miles away teach us to be ashamed. We veered away from our ancestral past, where our own spirituality was inseparable from how we lived, where we knew that Pele destroys and builds and Hi'iaka heals. *That's* the cycle of life our Hawaiian ancestors thought about."

He leans back, relaxes a tad, and shares an additional layer of his fury. "But my rebellion isn't just against religion. It's also about what that religion told me about my homosexuality. When I came here from Hawai'i, what was occupying my thoughts was the AIDS crisis," he says. "My partner, Bob, was working for the Shanti Project, and my friends were dying. Those were dark times. That contributed to my anger, but it's all related to what I'd been told as a child. All those years at St. Patrick's, praying—and I never felt inspired by Je-

sus. Think about Madonna. In her music and videos, she expressed her Catholicism with the imagery of S&M— black leather, lace, crucifixes, eroticism. I wanted to create my own version of that. I appreciate the rituals and the symbols of Catholicism—the singing, the clanging of bells, the incense. But the precepts? The dogma? Forget it!"

Things fell into place, he continues, after that day in his apartment when he read the missionary journals. The relentless rhythms of "Salva Mea," a song the British band Faithless had just released, which deals with the question of how to change the world, had been swimming in his head. It became part of the soundtrack for a suite of dances he called *The Natives Are Restless*. The production premièred on November 15, 1996, at San Francisco's Cowell Theater. In both subject matter and style, "Salva Mea" is the defining statement of Kumu Patrick's revisionist dance, which eventually gained the moniker hula mua.

Thematically, "Salva Mea" is about a nineteenth-century collision of cultures, a power struggle in which the harshest Christianity usurped Hawaiian beliefs and challenged the Natives' political power. It also deals with the legacy of that collision. We learn that Native Hawaiians continue to suffer in many ways. Their rates of poverty, infant mortality, life expectancy, and cancer are among the highest in the nation, and the most recent revival of their struggle for political power underscores, in a way, how much has been lost. Dance professor Angeline Shaka has called *Natives* "a hula performance with teeth," one that forces audiences "to confront

Pule (prayer), Cowell Theater, 1996

the painful (and ongoing) repercussions of Hawai'i's history of contact and colonization."

"Salva Mea" in particular draws on Kumu Patrick's personal experience of the Christianity that altered Hawaiian spirituality, allowing him to vent his anger at a repressive Catholicism that savaged the idea of homosexuality—and to condemn a society that chose to ignore the AIDS crisis. But hula mua, which he has developed over the past two decades into a bona fide style, allows him to use hula to make not just political statements but also artistic ones.

"There is a poem by Stephen Crane that I've loved since college," he says, searching for ways to explain the surprising darkness of some of his hula mua dances:

> In the desert
> I saw a creature, naked, bestial,
> Who, squatting upon the ground,
> Held his heart in his hands,
> And ate of it.
> I said, "Is it good, friend?"
> "It is bitter—bitter," he answered;
>
> "But I like it
> "Because it is bitter,

Opening of *The Natives Are Restless*, 1996

"Salva Mea"

"And because it is my heart."

As a choreographer, Kumu Patrick says, he needed a form of dance that would allow him to go to what he calls "the darker, turbulent places." A piece like "Salva Mea"—as well as other hula mua pieces—is an assemblage of unlike things (Kumu Patrick calls them "odd pairings"). The staging might recall a ballet or Broadway; the lighting might suggest the glow under the sea or the strobes on a dance floor; the costumes might pair the tight tank tops of the Castro district with the raffia skirts of the Cook Islands; the music might stir memories of the 1970s or recollections of your grandmother's living room. Kumu Patrick imagines the assemblage somewhat instinctively and designs it intentionally to express certain themes, but it often creates discordances that register on many levels with an audience and stir sometimes inchoate emotions.

Some of the individual pieces in *Natives* are fairly traditional—hula kahiko or hula 'auana accompanied in the usual ways, with dancers in the usual costumes—but the lighting, backgrounds, or staging may provide a tonal contrast. The broadest of the odd pairings may find traditional Hawaiian dance movements accompanied by non-Hawaiian music. This is, in fact, where Kumu Patrick's new style of hula originated. A few years before 1996, he used the Terence Trent D'Arby song "Sign Your Name" for a segment of a dance about Queen Ka'ahumanu and King Kamehameha. "The song has got tempo. It's got cadence," he explains. "And it conveyed the king's love for his queen just as effectively as any traditional Hawaiian chant."

But, especially in "Salva Mea," the pairings clash more than they complement, in keeping with the themes of disruption the dance explores. Gestures that may conjure swaying palms and soft shore waves are performed to hard-edged house electronic dance music. Robotic foot stamping is followed by arms that suddenly soften. A beat that is strong and staccato melts into something strangely fluid.

The effect is more like the layered structure of poetry than the linear thrust of prose. Different sensations hit the audience at once, and it's hard not to experience some combination of thrill, shock, brutality, wonder, and tragic loss. The dance screams, *This is not the hula you thought you knew.*

For viewers, the effect has not always been positive. Some audience members walked out of the original *Natives*, and some respected authorities on hula were downright uncomfortable with this California choreographer's break from tradition.

But many dance critics could tell that they had witnessed something ascendant. The *Los Angeles Times* praised the skill of the company and the inventiveness of its "visionary leader." The artistic director of the San Francisco Ethnic Dance Festival, David Roche, called it a work that "may some day be regarded with the same reverence as Alvin Ailey's *Revelations* or Martha Graham's *Appalachian Spring.*" And dancer and performance professor Angeline Shaka gave it a similar compliment in *Theatre Journal* by noting its broad appeal. "This progressive hula is angry, graceful, mechanical, new, old, urban, and rooted across multiple places and politics, including that of the queer/māhū hula dancer, the Native activist, and the showman all at once."

Kumu Patrick performed the piece again and again over the years—twenty times in San Francisco, six in Honolulu, and once in Long Beach. Each time, it evolved slightly. But by 2016, his own spirituality had evolved, and there were changes happening in Hawai'i, too, as the Native population was experiencing something akin to a second renaissance—this time as much political as cultural. So Kumu Patrick decided to reconceive the show, leaving certain dances intact, changing others, and adding an entirely new second act to address the issues now burning slowly through the islands like a finger of Pele's fire.

"Salva Mea"

"Maikaʻi ka ʻŌiwi o Kaʻala"

SAVE ME

Natives begins with a godlike voice cutting through the darkened theater. In a disgusted tone, a man quotes various missionaries, from the journals Kumu Patrick stumbled upon in his research. "Can these be human beings?" And the devil "looks about, rears himself up, and sniffs for the person he wishes to swallow." The curtain opens onto a stunning tableau of two dozen bare-breasted and elaborately tattooed women of all ages, shapes, and sizes, sitting regally onstage. Resplendent in bustled skirts, one layer of crisp cotton atop another, they perform a sitting hula with delicacy and beauty. (The combination of naked flesh and extravagant clothing is the first of the many visual clashes that mark the production.) The lights—shades of purple, gold, pink—glance off their bare arms and bare backs, which undulate gently in the darkness. One at a time, lone women call out a line of poetry; the others repeat it in unison and add more. Their chanting is throaty and proud, tender and melodious.

The voice that booms through the theater at the opening of *Natives*, decrying the "devil's nest" of hula, conveys anger and vindictiveness. But the women are the embodiment of grace. The disjunction settles on each audience member differently. Let's just say that few come out on the side of the missionaries.

The sense of discomfort only intensifies as the first act proceeds. The men perform a virile and compelling dance to the chant "Auʻa ʻIa" ("Hold Fast"). Their costuming—strips hanging from waist to knee in the front and back, folds of fabric sitting like clouds on their hips, crowns of spiky ferns—signals that we are

GOING TOPLESS

Kumu Patrick presented his vision for a new opening of *The Natives Are Restless* on a sleepy afternoon just before a performance of *The World According to Hula* in 1998. We had all just picnicked, and most of us had heavy eyes and were enjoying the sun. He started talking, telling us that next time he wanted to open *Natives* with us, the women, dancing topless, with tattoos scattered on our bodies. This was hula as our ancestors had known it before the missionaries came, and before nudity became synonymous with being a savage. It was a culture where the body was celebrated. He wanted to challenge the audience—had they bought into the idea that nudity was a bad thing, or were they going to be able to watch a dance to a love song and see it for all its beauty? He wanted to push the audience, to ask them to explore within themselves why they might feel uncomfortable in the face of nudity.

To some of us, the idea was distressing. But those who felt it was natural were onboard immediately.

I was hooked from the beginning. There was no way I was not going to do it. I have a profound trust in my kumu and knew he would never cast us in any unfavorable light. I could already see us dancing, with the lights slowly rising throughout the song.

However, being hooked did not mean that I did not have to overcome my own obstacles. Would my father be watching the show? What about my mother? My brother? Oh, they would deal with it; they would get it. But what about my body? I was overweight. How could I get onstage in this humble costume, the only one I had to offer? What if the audience believed what the missionaries have told us: that we should be ashamed of who we are? Then I stopped and realized that if I was having all of these thoughts in my head, every other woman in our group was, too. At this point, I let go and knew it would be OK.

Just before the opening of the show, we all tattooed each other, and the process engendered intimate trust. We had never been nude in the dressing room before, and we had certainly never touched each other's naked bodies. And here we were, dressing each other's skin with paint! Here was the acceptance I was looking for. I looked around, and all I saw was *life*: beautiful mothers, young women big and small, and people who had patterns tattooed on them by surgeons' knives. It was stunning, and it inspired me deeply. Every single woman had decided to do it. We questioned, trusted, let go, and accepted. We were now completely natural with the nudity and with each other. After we chanted together in a circle, holding hands, we went out to confront the audience. Did they see savages or the incredibly brave and beautiful women I saw in the dressing room?

—Makani da Silva

"Salva Mea"

still in ancient Hawaiʻi. Their words articulate a stirring message passed down for two centuries by the hula ancestors. It is the warning of the late-eighteenth-century poet, prophet, and chief Keaulumoku: "Hold fast, child, to your lands, your heritage," the chant urges; cling to your land and your identity in the face of a world turned upside down.

Then we are treated to the DJ-songwriter Moby, via his remix called "Walk with Me." It sounds almost like a twenty-first-century spiritual. Women, now in long black skirts and long-sleeved shirts, enter quietly, gracefully. The purple and blue gels pick up only the white of their shirts, exaggerating the sense that they are floating through the darkness. The music shifts to a choral hymn, a Hawaiian-language version of "The Lord's Prayer." The company of forty male and female dancers, buttoned up tight in their black-and-white clothes, mills about onstage. They turn to face the back screen, on which are projected portraits of Bingham and other missionaries who worked in Hawaiʻi between 1820 and 1848. One of the dancers plants a simple cross in the middle of the stage, right in front of the screen. Some hold their hands in prayer, some genuflect, some make the sign of the cross.

We have a church, a congregation.

A black-robed priest, played by Kumu Patrick, enters. He turns downstage and stops in front of the cross. The music shifts again, the urgent pulse of an electronic dance beat breaking the stillness of the worshippers. Daguerreotypes continue to pop onto the screen—missionaries fade in, fade out, and then are replaced by more, as insistent as the beat of the music.

The priest leaves, and the congregation gets to work, people dedicating themselves to the tasks they have

"Salva Mea"

by now been given: pounding nails, stacking wood, hoeing, washing. Their stillness has been replaced by a flurry of industry.

Then a voice calls out, "Yes!" and "Yes!" again—ecstatic, even orgiastic. The music changes, and the men and women are suddenly in a line all the way across the stage, stamping their feet in unison and moving forward. Think *Riverdance* without the clogs, the color, or the accordion. And without the joy: the dancers twitch their torsos left and right, summoning mechanical dolls more than angels of our better natures. At times they hinge at the waist, their arms zooming up behind them like demonic wings. (One writer compared them to birds of prey diving in an attack.) At times they merely move forward like a line of mercenaries, expressionless.

Then the priest storms angrily onstage, singles out one woman in the middle of the line, grabs her by the hair, and throws her over his bent knee. With a piece of charcoal, he marks her forehead with a cross, rips open her blouse, and brands her on her bare chest as well. Then, finished with her, he throws her to the ground and storms offstage. She struggles to get up and, now disheveled, stumbles back to the line.

She has been symbolically raped.

The dancers go back to their robotic but somehow eerily beautiful line dance.

The music shifts again, and they fall to the floor. Behind them is a line of brethren dancers, who have quietly arrived and stand in prayer. They look out over the front row of dancers at the audience, mute.

Then: mayhem. As the priest stands quietly by the cross, the congregants find pieces of charcoal and begin to defile each other. (The viewer's brain starts to fire: What is happening? Why have they turned on

"Salva Mea"

each other? Was the priest so persuasive?) They draw crosses on shirts, faces, and any other piece of skin they can find. They rip at each other, toss each other around like pieces of meat, push, grab, and throw each other to the floor. The conversion to Christianity has rippled through the Native Hawaiian population like a zombie infection.

In "Thank You for Hearing Me," the priest walks among female dancers, who by now have been defiled, their faces branded with lava-dark charcoal and their shirts torn. Blue lights, soft gels, and melancholy music impart a strange S&M overtone to the whole missionary mess, and the plaintive words of the song shudder with layers of paradox: "Thank you for hearing me. . . . Thank you for loving me. . . . Thank you for breaking my heart. . . . Thank you for tearing me apart. . . . Now I've a strong, strong heart. . . . Thank you for breaking my heart."

The priest, the very embodiment of fundamentalist fury, grabs the cross and holds it stiffly aloft, moving around the stage. The congregants follow their twisted Pied Piper. They do the hula equivalent of a bourrée, feet edging across the stage, hips twitching, torsos locked in place above the frantic footwork.

They continue to move in unison, sometimes raising their arms into Vs, sometimes lowering them to their sides, sometimes striking themselves on the chest with one fist. They move in a clump: stiff, then slumping; hard, then wilted. From an obedient crowd moving in unison as the priest directs, they turn into a clamoring mob as the lights go crimson—reaching for the cross, fighting one another, their arms a scrum, a scrimmage. Then the lights shift and the priest regains control. Then the lights shift and mayhem returns.

The movements themselves seem to have become disjointed; they have lost their grounding, like clock springs in an old cartoon that go suddenly haywire.

The priest climbs onto a mount behind the crowd and grabs the cross, and the dancers cluster below him, reverent again, a white circle of desperate arms, reaching for redemption in a tangle of ecstasy, fury, ferocity, and docility. A native population has gone from graceful to industrious to violent, from naked to neatly dressed to wandering around in tatters, from fiercely independent to strangely malleable.

The lights go black.

A CENTURY OF SADNESS—AND REDEMPTION

In 1993, when Patrick Makuakāne was starting his grand experiment with hula mua, he was responding—consciously, subconsciously, or stream-of-consciously—to stunning events across the ocean. The moment had a double meaning for Hawaiians.

On the one hand, they were looking backward in anger, marking the centennial of the overthrow of the Hawaiian Kingdom. The resulting suppression of native culture—of language, arts, and political power—had consequences that were still being felt. In 1993, only about 12.5 percent of the state's people identified themselves as "Hawaiians," and the language was on the brink of extinction. At the same time, six million tourists were arriving each year from the mainland and foreign countries, making the percentage of Native Hawaiians on the islands at any one time seem even more minuscule, and English (and perhaps Japanese) the language with currency.

But this was also a period of renewed Native pride. It was the time of ʻOnipaʻa, five days of performances, chants, and speeches about political and cultural sovereignty that culminated in a march of approximately fifteen thousand people from Honolulu's Aloha Tower to ʻIolani Palace. The former residence of Kalākaua

"Salva Mea"

and Liliʻuokalani was draped in black bunting to mark the occasion. But even if there was a heavy sadness in the people's hearts, words like "self-determination" and "steadfastness" were on their lips. Something new was emerging out of the cultural renaissance: a sometimes angry, sometimes dignified, sometimes jubilant, and always insistent argument that Native Hawaiians should have the same right to independence and self-government that had been granted to other Native American peoples.

It became known as the sovereignty movement, and it even had an urgent anthem: "Kaulana nā Pua" ("Famous Are the Flowers"), written as a protest song one hundred years earlier, expressing the Hawaiians' antipathy to annexation. It was often sung by late-twentieth-century singers with a fist raised high.

Hula, too, was gaining new life, resuming its station as a powerful, if subversive, cultural and religious touchstone and a wellspring of Native identity, much as Kalākaua had seen it one hundred years earlier. Students of Aunti Maiki and her contemporaries were training a new generation of kumu hula, as new hālau sprang up all over Hawaiʻi and the mainland. Young Hawaiians were flocking to these hālau, eager to reclaim their culture and find their own Native voices. Hula, whether as a choice in PE classes or as a serious academic subject, was being added to the curricula of both public and private institutions.

The annual Merrie Monarch Festival, started in 1964 in Hilo, was becoming known as the Olympics of Hula and drawing new audiences. And established kumu were expanding notions of where and how hula might be performed, beyond the "competition" model. In 1977, The Brothers Cazimero inaugurated an annual May Day show that ran for thirty years at the Waikīkī Shell and featured exquisite hula. The sisters Pualani

AN INCONVENIENT TRUTH

When most people think of Hawai'i, they envision beautiful beaches, lush mountains, and sunsets that could take the breath away. These alluring images are not false, but they amount to a public façade, and one that masks the tragic story of the Hawaiian people and their country.

The Hawaiian Kingdom willingly became part of the British Empire in 1794 and then was recognized by Great Britain and France as an independent state on November 28, 1843. As the only non-European power in the Family of Nations, the Hawaiian Kingdom was recognized as a neutral state and enjoyed equal treaties with the Austro-Hungarian Union, Belgium, Denmark, France, Germany, Great Britain, Italy, Luxembourg, the Netherlands, Portugal, Russia, Spain, the Swedish-Norwegian Union, Switzerland, and the United States.

By 1893, the Hawaiian Kingdom manned over ninety diplomatic posts and consulates throughout the world. Its government was a constitutional monarchy, and its citizenry enjoyed universal health care and education. The kingdom could boast of having a population whose literacy rate was nearly universal.

On the fateful day of January 17, 1893, the US diplomat assigned to Hawai'i ordered the landing of US troops to aid in the unlawful seizure of the Hawaiian government. Their goal was to transfer Hawai'i to the United States and secure Pearl Harbor as a naval base. Queen Lili'uokalani notified President Grover Cleveland of the involvement of US troops; on March 9, 1893, President Cleveland ordered a full investigation into the overthrow.

In his message to Congress on December 18, 1893, President Cleveland stated that the landing of US troops and the overthrow of the Hawaiian government was illegal, and he entered into a treaty to restore the Queen to her executive office. Despite his international duty to reinstate the Queen, political wrangling in Congress prevented him from doing so. Hawai'i was without a lawful government.

During the Spanish-American War, on August 12, 1898, the Hawaiian Kingdom was again invaded by the United States—an occupation that would last for over a century. After the war, militarization was unbridled; eventually, 118 military bases were established throughout the islands. Coupled with this militarization, a policy of Americanization in the schools prevented teaching in the Hawaiian language and sought to obliterate any memory of Hawaiian national consciousness.

As academic research has begun to uncover the truth about the occupation of the Hawaiian Kingdom, legal experts are taking affirmative steps to bring the occupation to an end under international law. The Hawaiian Kingdom will soon retake its place in the Family of Nations.

—Keanu Sai, PhD

Kanakaʻole Kanahele and Nālani Kanakaʻole, two kumu hula descended from a long line of famed chanters, created and choreographed *Holo Mai Pele*, a "hula opera," in 1995. (It later aired on PBS's *Great Performances*.)

FLOWERS AND STONES

Act I of the current version of *Natives* ends with "Kaulana nā Pua," the song popular with the sovereignty crowd and possessing its own fascinating history. A patriotic anthem protesting the 1893 overthrow of the monarchy, it was written by Eleanor Kekoaohiwaikalani Wright Prendergast, a lady-in-waiting to Queen Liliʻuokalani. The song is also known under the title "Mele ʻAi Pōhaku," the "Stone-Eating Song," because of a line in which the protesters say they find stones more palatable than the promises of the spurious new government (*Ua lawa mākou i ka pōhaku/ I ka ʻai kamahaʻo o ka ʻāina*: "We are satisfied with the rocks/ The wondrous food of the land.")

Kumu Patrick's focus on this "stone-eating" poetry springs from his knowledge of the ways in which Hawaiian music, chant, and dance have always done more than merely entertain. Hawaiian composers often use innuendo and metaphor to communicate clearly to certain listeners, while disguising provocative messages for others. The kaona, or hidden meaning, of many songs leads to a flower (*pua*) being used as a symbol for a secret lover. But in "Kaulana nā Pua" ("Famous Are the Flowers"), the blossoms are stand-ins for Native Hawaiian "children of the land."

Eleanor Prendergast

Those who speak Hawaiian recognize that Prendergast's "flowers" are hardly hibiscus or plumeria. "Famous are the flowers of Hawaiʻi," the song proclaims, and in doing so contrasts Native children with the "evil-hearted messenger" of the United States. The lyrics go on to insist that these children would rather "eat the stones of the land," and so nourish themselves, than be fed "by the government's hills of money" or by a colonizer's "greedy document of extortion."

In *The Hawaiian Journal of History*, scholar Amy K. Stillman gives recently uncovered details about the song. When the monarchy was overthrown in January 1893, members of the Royal Hawaiian Military Band—who were considered members of the military—were required to sign oaths of allegiance to the new government. A group of band members quit in protest on February 1. "We will be loyal to Liliʻu," they declared. "We will not sign the haole's paper but will be satisfied with all that is left to us, the stones, the mystic food of our native land."

Shortly afterward, Prendergast received a call from the group, asking her to compose a "song of rebellion." She complied.

For a century, "Kaulana nā Pua" was considered so precious that dancing to it was tantamount to disre-

Aloha 'Āina Unity March, Waikīkī, 2015

spect for Native Hawaiians. By 1970, Stillman writes, "that conception carried the force of an edict."

But in 1993, Stillman explains in her piece, a newly discovered article provided the perfect counter-argument—and catnip to Kumu Patrick. Two scholars revealed that in their extensive research, they found an account by Dr. Nathaniel B. Emerson, a historian and author of *Unwritten Literature of Hawaii*. In 1895, Emerson interviewed imprisoned counterrevolutionaries. According to one of the prisoners, the singing of the song on the first anniversary of the resignation of band members, on February 1, 1894, had "the effect of the 'Marseillaise' on the French. Not only did it excite and 'exasperate' them, but they 'beat out the rhythm, thumping their drums and miming their scorn of the 'paper of the enemy' [and] the 'heap of government money.'" Not only that, but they stamped their feet, twisted their heels, slapped their thighs, dipped their knees, and doubled their fists. In short, they performed the hula in the style, the prisoner said, of the Westernized hula ku'i.

Kumu Patrick read the account of this discovery with great excitement. What about a dance that paid homage to the prisoners, whose identification with the song was immediate and visceral? If ever a dance could mix gravitas and aggression, this was it.

RESTIVE NATIVES

When the curtain goes up for Act II of the new *Natives Are Restless*, the first tableau takes us to 2016 and

MOUNTAIN OF HOPE

Honolulu's Aloha 'Āina Unity March was not the only display of activism in the islands in 2015. The year also saw a cultural, legal, and spiritual victory by Native Hawaiians who stood down the state, the county, and giant national universities over control of the summit of Mauna Kea, Hawai'i's tallest and most revered volcano. What was remarkable wasn't the action itself: for the last forty-five years, Hawaiians have protested everything from the US Navy's bombing of the island of Kaho'olawe to the destruction of valleys for freeways and subdivisions. The surprising elements here were the organizational savvy and the swiftness of the victory. (It had taken decades to convince the federal government to end live-fire training exercises on Kaho'olawe, in 1990, then transfer the island to state jurisdiction, in 1994. Today, Kaho'olawe can be used only for Native Hawaiian cultural, spiritual, and subsistence purposes.)

A tremendous shield volcano on Hawai'i Island, Mauna Kea is the tallest mountain on Earth when measured from its base on the ocean bed. The summit itself, 13,796 feet above sea level, is an eerie expanse of red dirt, cinder, and snow. (The name Mauna Kea can be translated as "White Mountain," but the original moniker of the volcano was actually Mauna a Wākea, meaning "Mountain Child of Sky-Father Wākea.") It is whipped by wind, blanched by sun, and untouched by clouds that spread out below, interrupted only by expanses of ocean. On its slopes are some one hundred archaeological sites, most of them heiau, or shrines. And near the summit stands a cluster of enormous telescopes, including some of the most powerful on the planet.

In April 2013, the state Board of Land and Natural Resources approved construction of a Thirty Meter Telescope on Mauna Kea. The $1.4 billion observatory would operate as an international collaboration led by the California Institute of Technology and the

Mauna Kea

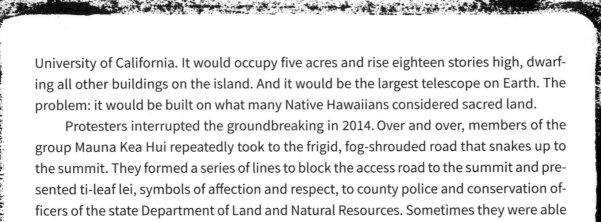

University of California. It would occupy five acres and rise eighteen stories high, dwarfing all other buildings on the island. And it would be the largest telescope on Earth. The problem: it would be built on what many Native Hawaiians considered sacred land.

Protesters interrupted the groundbreaking in 2014. Over and over, members of the group Mauna Kea Hui repeatedly took to the frigid, fog-shrouded road that snakes up to the summit. They formed a series of lines to block the access road to the summit and presented ti-leaf lei, symbols of affection and respect, to county police and conservation officers of the state Department of Land and Natural Resources. Sometimes they were able to turn away the trucks; other times they were arrested. They made news and persisted.

Opponents of the telescope were sometimes cast as superstitious natives battling science, but Kealoha Pisciotta, a former telescope operator on Mauna Kea and a spokeswoman for Mauna Kea Hui, disputed the characterization. "This is a very simple case about land use," she said, addressing the telescope builders. "It's not science versus religion. You're not Galileo. We're not the church."

In an October 2015 article in the *Atlantic*, staff writer Adrienne LaFrance describes the true stakes of the battle. "The fight over Mauna Kea is not just about a telescope, or even just about a sacred mountaintop. It is about the fate of a people whose land was stolen and whose cultural identity was desecrated, and almost destroyed, as a result. For those who believe native peoples have the right to determine the use of the land they originally occupied, even scientific progress on the grandest imaginable scale may not be enough to justify the construction of a telescope. In some ways, the question of what will become of Mauna Kea comes down to a decision about which loss is more bearable."

In December 2015, the State Supreme Court rescinded the construction permit for the telescope. In March 2016, a circuit court judge ordered the state to revisit the approval of the proposed telescope's land lease.

a stunning assembly of people. Lots of people. Multitudes. Filling the stage. Overflowing into the wings. They are dressed in the primary colors of protesters—who prefer to refer to themselves as "protectors"—now making a mark in the islands. They are indeed restless.

If they call to mind anything, it might be the masses who participated in the Aloha ʻĀina Unity March in August 2015, when ten thousand people crowded Kalākaua Avenue, turning Honolulu's tourist boulevard into a sea of red T-shirts, yellow banners, ti plants held aloft, and red-white-and-blue Hawaiian flags. Marchers stopped frequently to chant, sing, blow conch shells, and plead for their causes—from blocking telescopes on Mauna Kea, a mountain sacred to Native Hawaiians, to blocking GMOs on agricultural lands. In a way, it marked the next phase of the sovereignty movement in its focus on very specific issues relating to Native Hawaiian rights: issues like land use, water use, how to build a governing body for self-rule, and how to get banks and government agencies to use the Hawaiian language again after more than one hundred years.

Among the first words of the onstage protesters in *Natives* are the first lines of the contemporary chant "ʻO ke Au Hawaiʻi" ("Hawaiʻi in This Epoch"). In it, the composer, Hawaiian-language professor Larry Kimura, imagines a day when the descendants of the great chiefly clans of Hawaiʻi will rise up, proud of who they are as Hawaiians, and continue in the rich tradition of their ancestors. It begins, in the fierce *kāwele* style of chanting:

> *Auē e nā aliʻi ē o ke au i hala*
> *E nānā mai iā mākou nā pulapula o nei au e holo nei*
> *E ala mai kākou e nā kini, nā mamo o ka ʻāina aloha*

> O, the chiefs of the past,
> Look upon us, the descendants of this time
> Let us rise up, the multitudes, the precious children of the beloved land

"Woe to the stones that have been strewn and scattered," the chant goes on to say. "Let the rocks be restacked so that a new home foundation can be made firm." The mention of stones, of course, alludes to imagery in "Kaulana nā Pua."

Other dances in Act II celebrate recent efforts to rejuvenate the Hawaiian language and to restore fishponds near Kāneʻohe, an effort that combines ecology, economy, history, and culture in one fell swoop. There will be the "odd pairings" Kumu Patrick enjoys, including a Hawaiian-language translation of the Beatles song "Come Together," reimagined by Puakea Nogelmeier and again by Kumu Patrick. A piece praising ancient navigators will be paired with one praising the scientific stargazing that takes place at Mauna Kea. In Kumu Patrick's vision, science and stargazing might be able to coexist with cultural traditions—but on the right mountaintop, and as the choice of Native Hawaiians, not newcomers.

The new Act II, Kumu Patrick says, is intended to express the commitment of today's Native Hawaiians to a more complete cultural revitalization than was even imagined a generation ago. "We re-create an ancient fishpond to remind us how a community can be self-sufficient," he says. "We learn to speak to each other in our native tongue so that we don't have to tell our story in a foreign language. We understand that our kingdom was never annexed or colonized; we are still an independent sovereign state that is presently occupied."

In Act II, he adds, "We sing, dance, and shout not just our desire for self-reliance and self-government, but our determination to have it, whether in my lifetime or another."

"'O ka 'Au Moana"

"Lei Kapa ʻEhu Kai Kaʻena na ka Makani"

Chapter Six

Ka Leo Kānaka

("The Voice of the People")

"I hereby forbid all of you—foreigners, Chinese, and Natives—don't you folks let my Wahine Kāwika charge on my account. Because she has deserted our bed for no reason. She left of her own accord, and put the blame on me, as a means to entangle me with the laws of the land so that she may break our marriage vows."

So begins the saga of Mr. and Mrs. Kāwika, residents of Honolulu in 1862. As the voice of the aggrieved husband echoes, the browning page of a nineteenth-century newspaper, with a classified ad circled by hand, is projected over the proscenium stage at the Palace of Fine Arts Theatre. Those in the audience even slightly familiar with the Hawaiian language can follow the 1862 type, aided, of course, by the voiceover, which has translated it into English.

"Don't anyone grant her credit, lest your losses be heaped on her and not on me," continues the disgruntled husband, whose name, Kiope, we learn when he signs off "with affection."

mau aupuni ... o ke poo o ka Bipi, lio, hoki, miula, $1.00; no ke poo Puaa, kao, he 25 teneka; no ke poo Pelehu, moa, he 12½ teneka; koe nae ko na hoaaina, ke hele mawaho o ka pa aina. Mai hookuli oukou o ka poe mea holoholona, o pilihua ... oukou.

... ka manuwa ia he $1,774. ... a pau o ke ... kahiki eou ...

Luna kula, PIKA KAWIKI.

Honolulu, Iune 4, 1862.

OLELO HOOLAHA.

KE PAPA AKU NEI WAU IA OUKOU E NA Haole, a me na Pake, a me na kanaka maoli, mai hoaie mai oukou i kuu wahine mare ia Kawika, no ka mea, ua haalele kumu ole mai oia i ko maua wahi moe, a ua hele aku oia mamuli o kona makemake iho, me kona imihala wale mai ia'u, i wahi no'u e hihia ai ma ke Kanawai o ka aina, i hiki ai ia ia ke hooki i ko maua berita mare; ae no hoi! i noho no ka me ka pono ole, a imi hala wale iho no: Nolaila, mai hoaie oukou ia ia, o ili no auanei maluna ona ko oukou poho, aole maluna o'u. Me ke aloha huai pau no. KIOPE.

Ema Ruta moku, Hon. Iune 4, 1862. 37-3t

OLELO HOOLAHA.

O KA olelo hoolaha a Niheu, ma ke Hoku Pakipika, Helu 29, aole oiaio oia, no ka mea, aole no wau i haalele ia ia me ke kumu ole, aka, ua ike no ua Niheu nei, i ka hiki ole ia ia ke malama i ko maua ola oiai, e palupalu loa iho ana kona kino: Nolaila, ae mai no oia ia'u e imi no wau i ola no ko'u kino, a no kona ola pu hoi kekahi; a malaila no wau i keia manawa, e imi ana i ola, he wahahee ka hoolaha a Niheu. Owau no, PIIKU.

Iune 4, 1862. 37-3t

... OLELO HOOLAHA ...

---

e like me ke Kanawai, a pela no ke hoopoino, e ... na ia no ma ia Kanawai. Ua kapu loa ia Apana ... na holoholona a pau e like me maluna; a pela no kahi o Kalauki, Pake, ua kapu loa, mai hookuli poino auanei oukou.

AKEANA PAKE
AKIU PAKE
Luna o na Ilina Pake 34-6t

Honolulu, Mei, 15. 1862.

OLELO HOOLAHA.

E IKE na kanaka a pau, ua kapu ka lai, o W... lua, a me Koiahi; he mau Iliaina Kupono, ke Ahupua o Waihee, o Maui. Ua noa i na hoa... na e hele mau ana i ka hana a ke Konohiki, aole ... mea kuai dala. He $50.00, ka auhau no ka mal... hiki. E haawi ia Moo, me Kauwa.

S. M. KAMAKAU

Waihee, Mei 12, 1862. 35-5t

LIO NALOWALE.

MAMUA IHO NEI, UA NALO... LE kuu lio; mai ka pa o A... ka aku. He lio keokeo, me ka l... Wi D ma ka uha hope. O ka mea ... na e hoihoi ma ka pa o Alika, e uku ia no e like ka pono. Wm. DEDRICK

Honolulu, Mei 23, 1862. 36-3t

Ili! Ili! Ili!

E UKU aku no na mea nona na inoa malalo ... i ka uku oi loa no na ili, ke laweia mai ma ... akou hale kuai.

JANION, GREEN & Co

HEIHEI 6.—He puaa ua hamo ia ka huelo i ka aila. E alualuia, a ma ka huelo e hopu ai, e lilo ka puaa i ka mea e loaa ai.

HEIHEI 7.—He kia ua hamo ia i ka aila, o ... mea e pii ana a kau iluna, he puu dala kana.

He mau lealea e ae no kekahi.

O kela mea, keia mea, e makemake ana e hookomo i na Lio o lakou, e hele mai ia Kimo Pelekane (J. I. Dowsett,) ka Luna o ke kahua Heihei a e kakau i na inoa, me na heihei a lakou, manao ai e hookomo i na Lio, me ke dala pu mau no ka mea, ke puu dala manawalea kekahi i haawiia no kela heihei, keia heihei.

E pau ka hookomo ana o na Lio i ka 25 o Iune, mahope o ia i e hoolaha ia aku ana ka puu dala no keia heihei, a me kona Piula.

Luna o ke kahua Heihei.
KIMO PELEKANE, (J. I. DOWSATT.)

Na Luna nana o na Heihei.
D. R. VIDA, C. L. RICHARDS, Wm. DUNCAN,

Na Luna Hooponopono.
J. H. BRONN,
H. CORNWELL,
F. PRATT,
H. PRENDERGAST,
R. SELF,
J. L. LEMON,

---

linalina ma waena kohu o kona papalina akau, a ... ki i ka aos... na waha, ... ona poohiwi, he puu m... dala la ka nui.

W. C. PARKE.
Ilamuku Nu...

Keena Ilamuku, Hon. Iune 11, 1862. 38-tf

OLELO HOOLAHA.

E PEKU, A E KEKU AKU KA OLELO hoolaha a Kiope kuu kane mare, i hoopukaia ma ka Hoku Pakipika, Helu 37, o ka la 5 o Iune nei; e wahahee ana na'u ka ka haalele ia ia, aohe wahi mea a haalele o'u i ua Kiope nei, no ka mea, i ko maua mare ana, ua noho pu no maua no kekahi mau malaqus, aka, loaa wau i ka mai, ka hoomaka mai la no ia o ka haalele mai o ua Kiope nei ia'u, a noho pu aku me kekahi wahine e ma ke ano manuahi, a mahope iho, holo mai i Honolulu nei, a noho pu me kuu makuahine ma ke ano moekolohe, a kona wahine no ia a hiki i keia la. Ma ke Kanawai hea la o Alahe, o ko'u makuahine no oia no kana wahine? Aohe wahi mea a hilahila iho. Ua kii aku no wau e hoi mai maua, aka, aole nae o ia la malu mai, nolaila, hoopii au i mua o ka Lunakanawai, aka, ua loaa ko laua ola ma ka apua o ka olelo a na hoike. Ke hoolaha nei au, a puka kuu hoolaha ma ka Hoku Pakipika, alaila, e hele no wau e aie ma na Halekuai, a na Kiope, kuu kane mare no e hookaa oiai, aole i weheia ko maua berita mare. Owau no me ke aloha waianuhea. Mrs. KAWIKA.

Kaumakapili, Iune 12, 1862. 38-2t

WI MAKEMAKEIA.

H... ... PAONA WI I MAKEMA 21... Kek... manawa no, a e ukuia aku o na kene... ta ekolu no ka paona Wi hookahi me ka iwi no o wah..., a he elima keneta no ka paona hookahi, ke pau ka iwi i ka maihila. E lawe mai!

---

oukou, a e imi no i ke a... Ua lawa ko'u manao e ... ma ka hoike makahiki ma ... hai no au i na mea a pau ... Mai poina i ko oukou ... na palule o na ano a pau ... me, na holoku maikai, a ... ike ole ai mamua, a me ... E na makamaka, e li...

Hale Kua...

Aloha ouk...

JOHN
Kapaakiko, Aperila 1...

HALE HA...

KE HAI AK... na ka inoa malal... makamaka a me ke lehu... kuokuu hana i na ...

Kama Butt a...

o na ano a pau, me ka ... no ka mea, ua makauka ... ana i ka hana i na ...

KAMAA M...

Nolaila, ua hilinai oia ... na mea i na i ka makemak... ana e hele aku i kona w... Ma ke Alanui Hotele.

Honolulu, Aperila 24...

$1.50 W...

"Kandi"

Eight days later, Mrs. Kāwika gets her say. "Kick away and discard the announcement of Kiope, my husband," she says. Her voice, too, is projected out into the audience, and her own classified ad, in Hawaiian, replaces his on the screen. "He is lying that supposedly I left him. There is no way that I deserted Kiope, because, during our marriage, we lived together for some months, but I got sick. That was when Kiope left me, to dwell together with another woman in an adulterous setting."

Then the plot thickens: "After that, he settled here in Honolulu and also resided in the manner of adultery with my own dear mother, and she is his woman to this day. Nothing shames him. Tsa! Auē!"

Mrs. Kāwika will continue to charge whatever she wants at the stores, she warns, "and Kiope, my dear husband, will pay." Mrs. Kāwika signs off with a "yours truly, with sweet regards."

The newspaper fades out, replaced by a giant, abstract image of a green field with red, inkblot-like splotches and flowers looking like a cross between a pansy and a chromatography experiment. A woman is silhouetted against this backdrop. We get an opening chord, and then the few first bars of a ballad, and then the lights come up on Tanisha Reshke, a company soloist, in a sundress and a shell necklace. She is soon joined by five other dancers, then seven more, then another five. They dance to "Kandi"—a song by One Eskimo featuring a sample of Patsy Cline's "He Called Me Baby," sung by Candi Staton. (If that sentence makes your head ache, you get an idea of the complexity of the music involved.) The soulful lyrics—"It hurts beyond hurt" and "Does my love ever touch you?"—make a lyrical counterpart to the comical tit-for-tat of a nineteenth-century domestic squabble.

With that, the second act of *Ka Leo Kānaka* ("The Voice of the People") has begun. More on the first act in a moment, but Kumu Patrick's entire 2013 show takes its inspiration from the approximately one hundred Hawaiian-language newspapers that flourished in the islands from 1834 to 1948. This was an extraordinary phenomenon, especially considering that at the time, there were only around one hundred thousand people who

"He Mele no ka Nūpepa Kuʻokoʻa"

Puakea Nogelmeier and Kauʻi Sai-Dudoit are saluted from the stage at the San Francisco première of *Ka Leo Kānaka.*

could read Hawaiian. Credit for it goes largely to the young King Kamehemeha III, who had made literacy a prong of his three-decade-long rule. Thanks to him, according to Hawaiian-language scholar Puakea Nogelmeier, those one hundred newspapers constitute the largest indigenous-language corpus in the Western world.

And the newspapers weren't concerned with "just the facts, maʻam": they provided a kaleidoscopic image of Hawaiian culture and history. They contained accounts of lives extraordinary and ordinary. They recorded legal proceedings and business transactions, from land sales to charity contributions. They included stories about foreign lands, and they even set myths and legends in type and ran them as serials. The mastheads themselves were as exuberant as the content within, featuring Gothic script, sans-serif type, ships' sails, and animals with long tails.

But all of these stories, including the one of the quarreling Kāwikas, were hidden from the world for more than a century, available only to the few people able to read the Hawaiian language and willing to go into the bowels of libraries and sit for hours at microfilm stations. Only there—as well as in countless boxes squirreled away in museums and archives—would they find the newspapers that told the true history of Hawaiʻi. The entire collection was like a rich, fantastic message stuffed into a glass bottle and tossed out to sea.

NEW KNOWHOW

In 2011, a nonprofit educational organization in Honolulu launched a project to grab that bottle and uncork it. The organization was headed by Nogelmeier and his colleague Kauʻi Sai-Dudoit. They called the project ʻIke Kūʻokoʻa ("Liberating Knowledge"), and they had an outlandish vision: in a kind of "stone soup" for the

LIBERATING KNOWLEDGE

For decades, the 125,000 yellowing, molding, and increasingly fragile pages of the Hawaiian-language newspapers lay scattered among archives and libraries across the islands. By the 1970s, about seventy-five thousand of them had been put on microfilm. Meanwhile, the number of people who could speak Hawaiian, not to mention read it, dwindled. In the early 1980s, there were fewer than fifty Native Hawaiian speakers under the age of eighteen.

This was about when Marvin Nogelmeier arrived in Honolulu. The Minnesota native was on his way to Japan, but he fell in love with the islands and their culture and decided to stay. He has since become Puakea Nogelmeier, Hoku Award–winning songwriter, kumu hula, and associate professor of Hawaiian language at the University of Hawaiʻi. His PhD dissertation and first book, *Mai Paʻa i ka Leo* (*Don't Restrain the Voice*), revealed the overlooked but critical role of primary sources in Hawaiian history, including newspapers. Only 2 percent of the information contained in those newspapers has been integrated into the English-speaking world.

Nogelmeier has made it his mission to move this trove off the rudimentary reels of microfilm, out of the dark basements of university libraries, and onto the Internet, where it can be accessed by all, keyword-searched, and translated into English. Only then, he says, can it really transform our understanding of the history of Hawaiʻi.

What started as the Hawaiʻi Newspaper Project in 2000 became an ongoing effort, operated first through the Bishop Museum and then through Awaiaulu, a nonprofit educational organization directed by researcher Kauʻi Sai-Dudoit. A total of fifteen thousand pages were turned into searchable text and then made available on Web sites and public-access databases.

But Nogelmeier kept thinking about the untapped history contained in the sixty thousand pages still sitting on microfilm, forsaken. How to find people to do the tedious transcribing? Then it occurred to him: "What if I could find enough volunteers to turn the whole effort into a giant test of crowdsourcing?"

In 2011, he helped launch ʻIke Kūʻokoʻa ("Liberating Knowledge"), enlisting volunteers to transform all those images on microfilm into searchable pages of text. The task would be to view a snapshot of a page and type out all the Hawaiian words written there—no understanding of Hawaiian required.

In the end, about 2,700 people—from Hawaiʻi, the mainland, and twelve other countries—produced sixteen thousand typed-up newspaper pages. The forty-five thousand remaining pages were turned from digital images to searchable files using optical character recognition technology, which is less ideal than the manual product but still better than before. (It often turns century-old newspapers into what Nogelmeier calls "gibberish" and indecipherable "streams of letters.")

More than 240 of those 2,700 volunteers were affiliated with Nā Lei Hulu.

"Lei Mahiki"

In a number based on reports of the tragic death of the young prince Albert Edward, son of Queen Emma and King Kamehameha IV, Kumu Hula Shawna Alapaʻi performs a kanikau, or powerful form of lament, for the crown prince.

twenty-first century, they would seek volunteers from around the globe to digitize the thousands of articles, obituary chants, pictures, and literary epics. Once the microfilmed pages were typed into Microsoft Word, they could then be translated into English and searched from any computer on the planet.

Nā Lei Hulu i ka Wēkiu joined the project, hook, link, and SAVE button.

"Last year, we were part of an army of volunteers who took scans of Hawaiian-language newspapers and transcribed them into searchable typescript," Kumu Patrick tells his audience. He explains that Nogelmeier and Sai-Dudoit came up with the idea of a friendly competition in which high schools and hula schools, civic clubs and social clubs, universities and communities, would all compete with each other to see which one could transcribe the most pages.

"For a time, the top three kumu with the most student-typed pages were me, my hula sister Shawna Alapaʻi, and Oakland's Mark Hoʻomalu." He gestures to them or to other imaginary kumu, as if they were in the crowd. "You guys can win Merrie Monarch. We can win the newspaper challenge."

And win he did: Nā Lei Hulu transcribed almost 1,200 broadsheet pages, beating not just the other Bay Area hālau but every single one in Hawaiʻi, too.

The competition, it turns out, only spurred Kumu Patrick. The stories he read became the inspiration for *Ka Leo Kānaka* ("The Voice of the People"), the full-length show that premièred in San Francisco in 2013 and was performed in Hawai'i in May 2014. The show honors the quixotic project to upload a nineteenth- and early-twentieth-century outpouring into the digital universe. But it is also an homage to the newspapers themselves and to the poetic disposition of the Hawaiian writers, whose legacy is reframing much of what we know about nineteenth- and early-twentieth-century Hawai'i.

The papers' foreign news stories reveal a public curious about the world and aware of being an independent nation subject to the influence of other powers. Serialized romance novels and translations—of everything from *Tarzan* to *Twenty Thousand Leagues Under the Sea*—show a thirst for new forms of entertainment. Articles like "How a Woman Should Ride a Horse" mirrored the moral mission of Victorian-era newspapers around the world. Legal notices eloquently recorded the troubling story of the transfer of lands from Hawaiians to haole—literally "strangers," but, increasingly, white people. There were obituaries of royalty and rogues, sailors and seamstresses. And there were kanikau, the dirges loved ones wrote memorializing favorite moments with the deceased. When a royal died, there were many—but when a commoner died, a single kanikau might serve as an intimate obituary.

This source material gave Kumu Patrick the opportunity to become a dramatic storyteller of both the colloquial and the lofty. We get Mr. and Mrs. Kāwika—as well as disgruntled employees and angry ex–business partners—duking it out. We get a deity and her favorite "stud daddy." We get blind musicians. We get a telephone song written by a king. We even get two newspapers battling as furiously as competing hālau.

But the material is so rich, and spans so many aspects of the human condition, that *Ka Leo Kānaka* achieves a kind of universality as well. And, as in *The Natives Are Restless* and other works, its emotional power derives from its often dissonant blend of movement and subject matter. Hula hahiko, hula 'auana, and hula mua are all represented, as is a chunk of Hawaiian history. The added effects of sophisticated multimedia, unexpected lighting, and powerful contemporary music lead to unexpected associations, and sometimes even catharsis.

"The combination evokes a variety of emotions and asks questions," says dancer Ryan Fuimaono. "It makes people cry, and they don't know why. That's daring."

HAWAIIAN SIRENS

Act I and Act II of *Ka Leo Kānaka* both feature parts of an epic tale that ran in one of the nineteenth-century newspapers. It might be thought of as *The Iliad* and *The Odyssey* of Hawaiian literature, only it's about two sisters, instead of Greek men. It's the Pele-Hi'iaka story, and the women are the volcano deity, Pele, and her youngest and most adventurous sister, Hi'iakaikapoliopele ("Hi'iaka in the bosom of Pele"). The dances trace the journey of Hi'iaka and her companions, who make their way to Kaua'i, confront danger after danger, and find that their quarry, Chief Lohi'au, is dead. Hi'iaka must restore him to life and bring him back safely to her sister, the Queen of Fire.

Act I opens long before the Lohi'au part of the story, with a voiceover that explains the basics of Pele's arrival on Hawai'i Island from Kahiki, the invisible land beyond the horizon and the ancestral home of the gods—and also the Hawaiian word for Tahiti. After she ensconces herself on the island and falls asleep on the beach at Puna, Pele is awakened by the sound of a hula drum, which she follows to the island of Kaua'i. There, she captivates the royal court, challenges the wicked sorceresses of Kalalau Valley, and takes Chief Lohi'au as her own. Later, back on Hawai'i Island, she orders each of her sisters to find Lohi'au and bring him back to her home at Kīlauea. Only the youngest, Hi'iaka, obeys.

"E ka Mauli Ola"

The image above and on the facing page, as well as the one on the cover, depict Hiʻiaka and guardian spirits as they re-animate Lohiʻau.

After this recap, we hear the sacred pahu drum, as well as chanting that rumbles from deep in the chest. (The chanters in such dances always sit onstage, but in the shadows. The main voice is Kumu Patrick's, but he is often joined by other kumu or some of his students.) Eventually, the tone lightens as the ipu heke lays down a more fluid beat; the chanter strikes the gourd on the floor for a few beats, then creates intricate patterns by slapping the sides of the gourd either with his palm or with his fingers.

The first dances are precise hula kahiko, from a troupe that has developed as its trademark perfectly synchronized movement that rides the wave of the music, whether hula drum or Hawaiian guitar. The troupe has been compared to the corps of the Kirov and the Bolshoi, but that association does not account for the ferocity and power of these earthy dances.

The backdrop of the choreography is a sophisticated blend of multimedia. In the first suite of the Pele-Hiʻiaka dances, that backdrop shifts from blown-up watercolors of Native women to ragged lines of lava fire veining an obsidian field to mist to sepia-toned pages of century-old newsprint to clouds to the soft green fronds of ferns moving horizontally across the screen. The leaves of the ferns reach up toward the heavens and down toward the center of the earth, not unlike the upstretched arms and bare legs of the dancers onstage.

This part of the story of Pele and Hiʻiaka ends with men and women dancing over the still body of Lohiʻau, their voices and bodies rising and falling in waves, echoed in a chanter's voice. (The image on the cover of this book is a snapshot of this moment.) Then Lohiʻau's long limbs suddenly spring to life, just as the stage lights go dark.

"E ka Mauli Ola"

TURANDOT, WITH A TROPICAL TWIST

Kumu Patrick strolls back onstage, wearing a red patterned aloha shirt and black pants, with about six strands of white pīkake, or Arabian jasmine, around his neck. He introduces another legend, that of Lāʻieikawai, which appeared in serial form in two newspapers before it was published in a book in 1863. It is a romance centered on finding an appropriate suitor for a beautiful girl of high rank.

"In the quest to find a mate for Lāʻieikawai," Kumu Patrick tells the crowd, "the chastity issue is constantly put to the test. The men fail miserably. I think part of the problem is that there is no mediocre-looking person in this story. All the main characters are super hot! It's sort of like an ancient version of *Honolulu's Next Top Model* meets *The Bachelor*."

A high chief tries to woo Lāʻieikawai by sending his sisters, each of whom represents a different variety of the fragrant maile leaf. One by one, the sisters take turns trying to entice Lāʻieikawai with their unique fragrances. Over and over, the young ward is intrigued, but her guardian keeps convincing her it's just a ploy.

Kumu Patrick edges into Hawaiian Creole as he advances the story. "In the middle of a dark night, Lāʻieikawai is awakened by an alluring scent. Her guardian calls out, 'No get excited—it's that punk, trying for get you come down the mountain for marry him. You like marry him?'

"'No, I no like marry him.'

"'Then go back sleep!'"

Amid laughter, Kumu Patrick continues the narrative, which takes the reader from island to island, through boxing matches and surfing contests. Gods, chiefs, and prophets all play a part in courtly intrigue, as

"The Maile Sisters"

the search for a perfect suitor continues. In the end, Lāʻieikawai's family goes to the house of the sun to find the divine brother of the maile sisters. He agrees to marry Lāʻieikawai and whisks her off to the land of the rainbows, where they live happily ever after. "That is, until he meets her younger sister," Kumu Patrick adds.

The graceful dance that follows mixes killer kahiko and fluid ʻauana, and the music features two singers, an organ, and a percussion section. The women wear tea-length dresses, the men *lavalava*, or Samoan-style sarongs. They are all dripping in maile garlands.

THE BEACON

"Kauikeaouli is a pivotal figure," Puakea Nogelmeier says in a voiceover that introduces two numbers dedicated to the monarch who created what's come to be known as Hawaiʻi's Golden Age. The son of the great warrior who brought the eight inhabited islands of Hawaiʻi together under one rule in 1810, King Kamehameha III ascended the throne as a twelve-year-old, after the death of his father in 1819 and his older brother in 1824. Befitting his long name, Keaweaweʻula Kīwalaʻō Kauikeaouli Kaleiopapa Kamehameha, he was the longest-reigning monarch in the history of the Hawaiian Kingdom and is fondly referred to as either Kauikeaouli (pronounced *Cow-ee-kay-ow-oo-lee*) or Kamehameha III.

Some of this history is told in a video narration by Nogelmeier, some in an in-person narration by the ever-present Kumu Patrick. Both laud the king's most unusual effort: to encourage his people to read. Before 1820, Hawaiʻi was preliterate and had no written language. But then the missionary Asa Thurston and his cohort developed a Hawaiian alphabet, translated the Bible into Hawaiian, and started teaching people how to read it. Kamehemeha III was one of their first students. Not only did the young king quickly learn to read and write, but he chose to make universal literacy a part of his legacy. "*He aupuni palapala koʻu* ('mine will be a nation of literacy')," he declared in his first speech to his people, on June 6, 1825. A generation and a half later, almost 100 percent of his subjects made good on his words.

Nowhere is this embrace of literacy more apparent than in the Hawaiian-language newspapers that sprouted up in the next century. They proliferated like *naupaka* shrubs on the beach; more than 125,000 pages of Hawaiian-language newspapers were printed in more than one hundred different papers over 114 years. The first, *Ka Lama Hawaiʻi*, appeared in Lahainaluna on February 14, 1834. (Its name can be translated as the *Beacon*.) The second, *Ke Kumu Hawaiʻi* (the *Hawaiian Educator*), came just months later, on November 12, and was published in Honolulu.

And Kamehameha III's literacy campaign was part of a larger effort to bolster Hawaiʻi's sovereign identity. He wanted his country to be self-governed, so he established a house of representatives, a constitution, and a supreme court. Eventually he succeeded in having his island kingdom recognized as a sovereign state by many countries, including England, France, and the United States.

Kumu Patrick joins seven men and eight drums onstage for the first number honoring this influential leader. It's a nineteenth-century men's drum circle, meant to remember the way Kamehameha III let the missionaries know he wouldn't bend completely to their practices. The dance that follows, with shouting, hip gyrations, and more, would have impressed Elvis Presley. It honors Kaomi, a young man in the king's party bunch who was an especially intimate companion.

Onstage monologue

LAVA SANDWICHES

In Act II, Kumu Patrick resumes the narration of the Pele-Hiʻiaka story, or, as he calls it, "Peleʻs infatuation with Chief Lohiʻau." He says this with a sly smile—not to mention a nod to his very San Francisco audience, which may have a distinct appreciation for Chief Lohiʻauʻs appeal. "This man is renowned for his handsomeness," Kumu Patrick continues, upping the ante. "A stunning specimen. He goes to the gym every day, he plays the hula drums, heʻs an amazing hula dancer, heʻs the emcee of the luau, he probably decorated the hall.

"All of this, and heʻs still a heterosexual!"

When the crowdʻs hoots and hollers subside, Kumu Patrick goes back to his tale, reminding us that back in Act I, Hiʻiaka "was working her Hawaiian voodoo magic and bringing Chief Lohiʻau back to life."

The devoted younger sister, remember, has been tasked with escorting Lohiʻau back to the island of Hawaiʻi—and to Pele. On the way, omens in the sky tell her that Pele has killed her best friend and destroyed her lehua garden. All this because Big Sis is jealous that Hiʻiaka had a dalliance with a man on Oʻahu before heading to Kauaʻi. "Hiʻiaka apparently didnʻt get that memo," Kumu Patrick says, alluding to the fact that Pele cannot stand it that her sister is so attractive to men. And this was before she even met Lohiʻau.

"True"

So, of course, on the way back to Hawaiʻi Island, Lohiʻau and Hiʻiaka act on their intense attraction for each other. (Apparently, says Kumu Patrick, he's suffering from a severe case of Stockholm syndrome and she's suffering from a severe case of "holy moly, this guy is hot!")

Then they get back to Hawaiʻi Island. So furious is Hiʻiaka about Pele's destruction of her best friend *and* her lehua garden that she decides to make passionate love to Lohiʻau at the edge of the crater, in full view of Pele. Odysseus's sirens have nothing on this Hawaiian dame.

"Back in the pit of Kīlauea," Kumu Patrick intones, ratcheting up the drama, "Pele patiently waits for Hiʻiaka. Her other sisters look up and say to Pele, 'Eh, *hui*, try look up there. She stay with your boyfriend. And now she kissing your boyfriend.'

"Pele's like, 'Oh, no, it's probably just a peck on the cheek—they're saying goodbye.'

"The sisters' chorus continues: 'Now they taking off their clothes. Now she on top of him. Oh, and now he on top of her.'"

Kumu Patrick pauses, then continues. "It gets very Jerry Springer from that point on—hot and steamy at the crater's edge. A few chants later—bam!—Lohiʻau is a lava sandwich."

DANGEROUS

That could be the end of the Pele-Hiʻiaka story. But it's not. "Little Sister is a mess," Kumu Patrick says. "She runs away to the underworld. Lohiʻau is dead again. The mood at the volcano is pretty crappy." But Pele's older brother comes to the rescue, restoring Lohiʻau to life, convincing Pele that she and her sister were both wrong, and encouraging the Hawaiian equivalent of "forgive and forget." Kumu Patrick continues, "Pele finally agrees and sends Lohiʻau off to find Hiʻiaka so that he and she can live happily ever after for a couple of months. Lohiʻau finds his beauty on the island of Oʻahu, where they open the floodgates of passion."

Kumu Patrick wraps things up and starts to move toward the wings: "Hiʻiaka's dangerous sojourn ends," he says. "It's been a long, laborious journey battling demons, ghosts, and assorted ne'er-do-wells, but in the end she finally gets her man. The moral of the story? Never send your gorgeous younger sister to fetch your boyfriend when he's on another island. Jump in that canoe and get him yourself!"

Kumu Patrick leaves the stage, and a young man and woman replace him—he in black shirt and brown pants, she in a red spaghetti-strap dress, her long black hair held back by a giant scarlet flower. Their duet, to a remix of Michael Jackson's "Dangerous," is one part hip-hop, one part Broadway, one part hula. The dancers' naked arms make sharp lines and hard angles. They twist, they turn. They look toward each other, they look away. The lyrics fit: "As she stalked the room/ I could feel the aura / Of her presence." The female dancer, Kahala Bishaw Fisher, is indeed both "persuasive" and "dangerous."

Kumu Patrick adds one more potent ingredient to the "Dangerous" mix. Twice, snippets of Aunti Maiki's chanting part the waters of the Michael Jackson song. First, she chants "Mai Kahiki ka Wahine ʻo

Who would put "hula" and "jazz" together in the same sentence, not to mention the same performance? The truth is, Hawai'i had its jazz moment. Gabby Pahinui was renowned for playing in that style before he gained fame as the god of slack-key guitar. And Louis Armstrong, with Andy Iona, recorded an album called *Jazz Goes Hawaiian*. *Ka Leo Kānaka* features four numbers inspired by the Jazz Age. A segment called "*Kalapu Jazz*" is based on advertisements for a band composed of blind musicians. "TA-HU-WA-HU-WA-I," above, uses the title Andy Iona gave to one of the songs.

Pele" ("From Kahiki Came the Woman Pele"), the chant that earlier opened the show. Then she chants a verse from "Pu'uonioni," a hula taught to all students in Nā Lei Hulu. The dancers slow down, as if hypnotized by the ancient music, and their hip-hop melts into hula kahiko. Then—snap!—they return to their furious duet.

As is often the case in Nā Lei Hulu shows, one dance flows into another: the woman in red is now joined by a group dressed just like her, though in different colors. "True"—a remixed, mostly instrumental version of the 1980s hit by Spandau Ballet, the song of many a senior prom and part of the soundtrack to movies like *Sixteen Candles*—form the music for an all-female dance, interspersed with bits and pieces of various chants about Hi'iaka and Lohi'au, performed in aching voices by Kumu Patrick, Jason Laskey, and Ryan Fuimaono. It is nuanced and lovely where "Dangerous" was sizzling hot.

NEWSPAPER SONGS

Kumu Patrick comes back onstage one last time to set up several numbers about the newspapers and the voices they expressed. It wasn't just Mr. and Mrs. Kāwika who duked it out in the papers, he tells us. "For three consecutive years, from 1861 to 1863, there was an intense rivalry between *Ka Hōkū o ka Pākīpika* and *Ka Nūpepa Kū'oko'a*. You weren't considered a serious newspaper if people didn't write songs about how great your paper was, saying how it points to truth and integrity and fills subscribers with joy. But the newspapers wrote songs about themselves, too. They even talked smack about each other: 'That other newspaper is like a leaky house with a kaka-roach in the corner!'"

The audience response suggests everyone gets the joke, recognizing the Hawaiian Creole version of "cockroaches." Then Kumu Patrick turns serious. "*Ka Nūpepa Kū'oko'a* is the granddaddy of them all," he says with respect. "It published from 1861 to 1927—the longest running of all the Hawaiian-language newspapers. Its song says, 'Chiefs and officials,/ Teachers and students,/ Compatriots in righteousness,/ Let us all stand together for the Independent Kingdom.'"

Kumu Patrick ends his narration with "*E ola nā ali'i a me ka nūpepa kū'oko'a!*" ("Long live the royalty and the independent newspaper!") He steps offstage, making way for two final, lively dances. The first is to a song written in 1883 by King David Kalākaua, about a newfangled instrument introduced to the Hawaiian Islands: the telephone. (The King had one installed immediately, so his palace was wired several years before the White House.)

The last song of the show is "He Mele no *Ka Nūpepa Kū'oko'a*," or "A Song for the *Newspaper Kū'oko'a*." (That last name, by the way, also means "independence.") The pride of a people who were early adapters of the telephone, electricity, and especially literacy is echoed in this last number, in which dancers enter the stage in costumes printed with old newsprint. They carry broadsheets (actual facsimiles of a *Kū'oko'a* newspaper) and make them part of the dance.

Of course, the real-life ending to the newspaper story isn't so upbeat. In many ways, its fate paralleled that of the Hawaiian language. In 1893, when Queen Lili'uokalani was arrested and overthrown, the Hawaiian-language newspapers were filled with accounts of the events. In 1896, a new law making English the language of instruction in government and private schools appeared—in both English and Hawaiian. If Lili'uokalani's overthrow was the death knell for the Hawaiian Kingdom, the new law was the death knell for the Hawaiian language. The reading continued, but, more and more, it was in English.

"He Mele no ka Nūpepa Kūʻokoʻa"

Blame it on missionaries, blame it on Machiavellian figures, blame it on the Jazz Age or other encroachments by the mainland, but whatever the reason, the fact is that through the first half of the twentieth century, the number of people who could speak and sing in Hawaiian, not to mention read in it, was dwindling. By 1950, that number plunged into low five figures.

By then, the boisterous Hawaiian-language newspapers had fallen silent. The last one, *Ka Hoku o Hawaiʻi*, out of Hilo, ceased printing in 1948.

But the message of *Ka Leo Kānaka* is hardly elegiac—or even sad, really. In the story of the Hawaiian-language newspapers, lost in the twentieth century and recovered in the twenty-first, Kumu Patrick finds a "voice of the people" that almost disappeared, perhaps, but that today is growing more textured and intriguing. The recovery of a trove of molding pages has inspired a show that tacks between deities and demons, lovers' squabbles and amorous trysts, the words of a mellifluous ancient tongue and the words of a guttural Creole still spoken in the fiftieth state.

The message about that Hawaiian voice is a message about the hula as well. Aunti Maiki Aiu Lake has slipped into the show obliquely, as the voice of the chanter in "Dangerous." And yet she is here in spades, for *Ka Leo Kānaka*, with its range of motions and emotions, animates not just some old newspapers but her motto: "Hula is the art of Hawaiian dance expressing all that we see, hear, feel, taste, touch, and smell."

"Ke Kumu o ke Ola," honoring the Hawaiian patriot Robert Wilcox

"Born This Way"

PART III

I Mua ("Moving Forward")

Where is hula at the dawn of the twenty-first century? And where are Hawaiians? Both questions inform the current work of Kumu Patrick Makuakāne. Nā Lei Hulu celebrated its thirtieth anniversary in 2015, and the hālau is today as buff and boisterous as its leader. The troupe performs to sold-out audiences, and hula mua, rejected by purists in Hawai'i when the dances débuted, are practically accepted as part of the canon—or at least his canon. And while what's become known as "the diaspora" was just beginning when Kumu Patrick first arrived in California, now more than eight hundred thousand Native Hawaiians and Pacific Islanders make the mainland home and eagerly embrace his syncretic style.

Kumu Patrick continues to stretch the aesthetic boundaries of hula, incorporating themes about Native Hawaiian identity but also choreographing dances that refer to San Francisco much as an older hula might praise a specific mountain peak or an expanse of coastline. He also continues to stretch the reach of his hālau—not just as a company, a school, and an arts organization, but as an *'ohana,* an extended family for the many people the hālau touches. It's all part of a larger mission to find inspiration in traditional knowledge and cultural practices and then reinterpret that information for an increasingly global audience.

"Lepe 'Ula'ula"

CHAPTER SEVEN

Kanakolu

("Thirty Years")

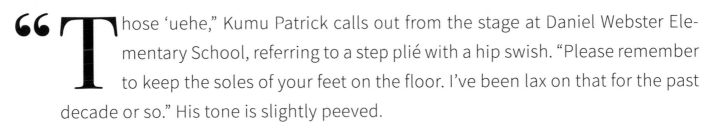

"Those 'uehe," Kumu Patrick calls out from the stage at Daniel Webster Elementary School, referring to a step plié with a hip swish. "Please remember to keep the soles of your feet on the floor. I've been lax on that for the past decade or so." His tone is slightly peeved.

The dancers in his performing group are running through their warm-up. The kumu holds out his right hand and taps his fingers, one by one with the left, as if playing "this little piggy went to market." He begins: "I can tell who practiced [index finger], who didn't [middle finger], who thinks they don't need to practice [ring finger], who needs to practice [pinky]. I know, you say to yourself, 'I never thought I had to practice'—and some of you don't. But if you don't practice and you come to hula, you'd better be *fabulous*."

It's a little past noon on a Sunday in February 2015, and Kumu Patrick is leading company practice in the "downtime" of the year, between the big shows that happen each October. This time they're rehearsing *Kanakolu*, their thirtieth-anniversary show, which is a kind of "greatest hits" of Kumu Patrick's dances: perennial crowd-pleasers and bits of choreography that have, over thirty years, become known as the hālau's signature pieces.

"The Gift"

(The critics sometimes differ from the crowds on such repertory shows. In 2007, Jennifer Dunning, of the *New York Times*, mused about whether "Mr. Makuakāne's genial between-numbers banter has grown somewhat weary-sounding and too practiced" and whether the "novelty of seeing traditional-style Hawaiian dancing to music by Peggy Lee, Cyndi Lauper, and Tony Bennett" didn't wear thin after a while. Though he doesn't mention such feedback, Kumu Patrick is clearly bent on answering such critics with riveting dancing.)

Thirty-five of the company dancers are lined up in six rows, some in sweats, some in skirts with elastic casings that gather volumes of cotton around the hips. Many of them are professionals in fields as diverse as massage therapy and banking, and Sunday is their lone rehearsal day of the week. Which may explain Kumu's particular teaching style. To make it perfect, to get everyone to perform together in a cohesive unit, you *have* to be exacting. "He's much more forgiving of his dancers now," says Makani da Silva, who started with him as a child. She still remembers him taping her hands to keep her fingers from splaying.

"He has his moods," notes Debbie Garcia, who, as the *alaka'i*, or assistant teacher, in the hālau, watches him from a close remove. She clearly respects that, unlike many kumu, he teaches as many classes as he can. "As kumu, he plays multiple roles: the nurturer, the artistic director, and the critic."

Even as a benevolent patriarch, Kumu Patrick remains a perfectionist. These may be the crème de la crème of his school, but he still pulls out every stop, scolding, badgering, inspiring, making metaphors, and giving a little hula history to help his troupe grasp not just the moves but the meaning. And not just the meaning but the feeling.

Nā Lei Hulu beginner class

Kumu Patrick is barefoot onstage, dressed in board shorts and a worn black T-shirt that says JEET KUNDO on the front, superimposed over an image of Bruce Lee, with red-and-white kanji characters on the back. He often starts the Sunday warm-up the way he starts every class he teaches, and the way his kumu did, by taking dancers through each of the ten basic steps of hula. The exact number of steps is an issue of great debate among hula dancers, but he sticks to ten for the warm-ups. (In the approximate order in which he teaches them, they are *kāholo, kāwelu, kā'ō, hela, lele, 'uehe, lele 'uehe, 'ami, 'ami kūkū,* and *'ōniu.* Occasionally he adds one more, *'ai kāwele,* if it comes up in a dance. There are still others that only the performing company learns.)

Kumu Patrick almost invariably follows the warm-up with his own version of "Kāwika," the song praising King David Kalākaua that is a standard in all hula schools. After a few other standards, he turns to the numbers he is teaching his dancers for the next show. Because these are early rehearsals, he is not yet using his pahu drum. Instead, he stands behind a wooden lectern, banging it with a ferocity that would make even the Daniel Webster Elementary School principal cower.

He pounds out the beat for "Ho'olono 'Ia Aku Ho'i Kaua'i" ("Kaua'i Has Now Been Heard"), a mele composed in honor of King Kalākaua's birthday jubilee on November 16, 1886. He has choreographed it as a slow, deliberate dance, with grand sweeps of the arms, subtle tilts here and there, and a few strong and swift motions to punctuate the others.

"That 'āina," he says, stopping and referring to the word for "land" and to a moment where the arms move quickly from pointing groundward (along with the entire torso) to hinging in front of the chest,

"Lights"

Intermediate classes, Hōʻike Nui, 2014

parallel to the ground, as the torso unbends. "When you come up, it's a nice, soft lift," he barks, then softens. "Sometimes you imagine a lift, but your *kino*, your body, doesn't actually lift. But if you imagine it, the lift is there. Think about cinnamon and the whiff of fragrance it gives. You don't dump it into your cookies. It must be soft."

He continues, launching into a sermonette he repeats over and over, not just in beginner classes but with these company veterans, too. "Old hula like this are very simple, not too many motions," he begins. "The story is not in the hand—the story is in the mele. Because we lost the language, our hula movements became more dramatic."

With those last words, he thrusts both arms into a dramatic V to demonstrate. "It's not this, either"—he bends his elbows and makes his palms like a Balinese dancer. "Or this"—he kicks in a parody of a cancan girl.

Most songs from the past two centuries have a rhythmic refrain, a sort of caesura in between verses, called a *pā*, which allows the dancer a chance to go on autopilot for a few seconds—to collect the self and get ready for the next verse. The pā for "Hoʻolono," however, is hardly a rest. The arm and leg extend to one side at a forty-five-degree angle, jutting out, tucking in, then jutting out again, while the torso bends to that side and the opposite arm extends upward. Oh, and the hands rotate forward and back, along the axis of the arm. Think triangle pose in yoga, only your hand isn't resting on your shin, you don't get to hold the pose, and your palms are rotating to the beat.

"In this pā, you are really working," Kumu Patrick says. Then he plunges the knife in: "But you cannot look like you are working."

Patrick Makuakāne & Nā Lei Hulu I Ka Wēkiu present

THE HULA SHOW 2011

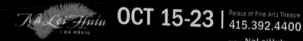

OCT 15-23 | Palace of Fine Arts Theatre
415.392.4400
www.NaLeiHulu.org

Practice continues, and he keeps up a constant patter—partly to motivate his dancers, partly to give them tiny rests, partly to coax virility and femininity out of a group of people of varying body types, ages, and sexual preferences: "Gents, don't get *moloā*," he admonishes, using the word for "lazy."

"Ladies, that's an easy lean—not a tango move. Like this." He tilts backward gently.

"*Hiki nō?*" In other words, "Got it?"

"Boys, what is *that*? Are you doing a man hop?"

He turns over the teaching of "If I Could Be with You," a seductive female dance set to the song by Louis Armstrong, to three of his veteran dancers. They watch, critique, and coach the others. "Some of us—maybe I'm one—look like we are doing shoulder exercises," says Janet Auwae-McCoy. "You're not stretching your sore neck here! You are being sexy."

"The feminine mystique," he says admiringly, as he watches. "Some have it, some don't."

Eight months later, when *Kanakolu* is performed, the dance critic Allan Ulrich comments in his *San Francisco Chronicle* review on the results of such painstaking rehearsals. Perhaps Kumu Patrick's singular accomplishment, he suggests, has been "to weld a group of committed part-time dancers into a troupe that moves with a singular impulse. When these 37 dancers fill the stage with impeccable swaying unisons and pelvic rotations, and delight us with a complex gestural language, you begin to wonder where amateur ends and professional begins."

CELEBRATING THREE DECADES

The *Kanakolu* performance begins with *Mālamalama ʻO Kapalakiko* (*Shimmering Is San Francisco*), a suite based on a collection of chants composed by language professor Puakea Nogelmeier. First performed in 2011, the chant collection speaks to the long-standing connection between Hawaiʻi and the City by the Bay. Between the lines, it celebrates the home of Nā Lei Hulu i ka Wēkiu. As Nogelmeier often reminds his students, an important genre of Hawaiian poetry is the mele ʻāina, or song celebrating a place. These particular mele ʻāina glorify the California metropolis for its art and skill, recognize its embrace of high chiefs in the nineteenth century, find the nuances in its mists, and even honor the hālau's home turf of Potrero Hill.

In a multimedia montage that forms a backdrop to the dancing, photos of the Golden Gate, the fog, the bridges, and the familiar line of Victorian homes on Alamo Square are juxtaposed with illustrations of Hawaiian figures, pictures of lava flows, and sunlight filtering through the sea. (Such backdrops have become as much a part of Kumu Patrick's staging as the dramatic lighting. They are designed by projectionist Marty McGee, whose day job at Animated Architecture has him designing and operating shows in hotel ballrooms conferences, stadiums, and arenas.)

The crowd favorite in this collection is dedicated to San Francisco crab. The dance is classified as a hula maʻi, or fertility dance. It extols the dynamic sexual energy of scurrying crabs—and the heaven-on-Earth feeling of opening them up and indulging in their sweet meat.

"You do know that Hawaiians love to eat crab, right?" Kumu Patrick asks the audience when introducing the dance. "This chant says, *Heed my call, o great crab, crawling along the sea floor, powerful form in a hard shell, as you seek your way to the trap.*" He continues, gesturing forcefully, beckoning to an imaginary crustacean, and understanding that many in the theater realize that in Hawaiian songs, any reference to eating something specially prepared and dripping with juices is just a metaphor for piquant foreplay.

"He Mele Pāpaʻi"

Kumu Patrick plays to those in the hall who are in the know: "Desire is what drives you here; now you're caught and held fast. Heed my call, o great crab—here you are, right in front of me, flipped on your back and buttered up."

It might be argued that every hula is, in one way or another, about sex. But some of Kumu Patrick's signature dances are definitely about something else—pure nostalgia, perhaps, or a bit of melancholia dressed up and made beautiful.

In his onstage patter, he indulges in a little reminiscence about some of these outliers. "For the fiftieth anniversary of the recording of 'I Left My Heart in San Francisco,' we had the privilege of performing at city hall for Tony Bennett," he notes. "That was a disaster. Note to self: never assume that three choral groups banding together would actually sing Mr. Bennett's song like the recording. Train wreck for hula dancers!"

Not all his performances with celebrities have been disastrous, though. The troupe danced "First Time Ever I Saw Your Face" in a show with Roberta Flack at the War Memorial Opera House on February 14, 2011. "When we first rehearsed it with her," Kumu Patrick remembers fondly, "she looked away and said, 'I can't watch this. It's too beautiful.'"

THE FIRST TIME EVER I DANCED WITH ROBERTA FLACK!

How I wanted to pull my camera from the pocket of the jeans beneath my pāʻū (practice skirt).

At the end of a line of dancers, during rehearsal, I snuck a peek to my left and could see all my hula sisters dancing in unison, bodies dipping and arms rising to the music. Beyond them, singing at the piano, was the legendary Roberta Flack.

"Just one snap!" I thought. "What a memento." I didn't dare.

Twenty minutes earlier, Ms. Flack had breezed into the theater with her entourage and taken control of the rehearsal. She kept her sunglasses on the entire time. "Why are they dancing over there?" she burst out. "Because of the lights? They should be over here. I want lights here!"

Whoa, she doesn't mess around.

We were so nervous. Even though we'd danced to her renowned recording of "The First Time Ever I Saw Your Face" a million times before, the unpredictability of *live* music could throw off even the most seasoned ensemble. And *this* live music was coming from Flack's own mouth—a truly surreal experience.

Apparently things went well, because as soon as Flack started to watch us, she said, "Oh, I can't even look at you—I'm gonna cry," and promptly turned away.

She liked it! What a relief. Still, we couldn't be sure the show would go smoothly. We retreated backstage and, accompanied by a recording we'd surreptitiously made during rehearsal, ran through the piece again and again. But who knew if she'd even sing the song the same way that night? The anxiety was palpable.

Finally, it was showtime. Flack toyed with the melody and phrasing, letting the words surge and slow, but the basic beat held steady. We clung to it like a life raft, intent on moving together. Luckily, our concentration left little mental space to register the magnitude of the moment.

After the show, Flack came to us and asked coyly, "How can I bring you with me everywhere I go? I feel the emotion of that song every time I sing it, but with your dancing . . . it really enhances what I feel."

We knew she meant it. She doesn't mess around.

—Jenny Des Jarlais

"Birth Certificate Hula"

When he first presented hula mua like "First Time," Kumu Patrick earned a bit of a reputation as a bad boy of hula. Some experts and elders considered him a showman, his style "too theatrical." Since then, he has gained a few bona fides, not to mention packing performance halls and garnering attention from mainland critics. And, of course, earning the sanction of Aunti Mae Klein during his 'ūniki, which gave him the hula equivalent of a gold medal and a brass ring, all wrapped in a blue sash.

Which isn't to say his dances aren't intentionally mischievous. Give him a subject, any subject, and he may well poke fun at it. Take the controversy over the birthplace of Hawai'i's first "native son" president, Barack Obama. That gave us "The Birth Certificate Hula," which begins by teasing those who need a lesson in geography: "We're a long way from Africa/ Honolulu doesn't look like Kenya/ So you have to do . . ./ 'The Birth Certificate Hula.'"

Or consider "The Hawaiian War Chant," originally penned as a love song in the 1860s by Prince Le-leiōhoku, the brother of Kalākaua. English lyrics were written in 1936 and the tune was changed by Johnny Noble, the king of *hapa-haole* (literally "half-white") music. This bastardized version of the prince's song, often renamed "TA-HU-WA-HU-WA-I," has been performed by Tommy Dorsey, the Muppets, and Hawai'i's first comedienne of hula, Hilo Hattie. In Kumu Patrick's choreography, women in slinky white and men in dress black do the Charleston, the Watusi, and anything in between. Their hula is pretty close to the movements performed by the most unknowing dancers, whose hips swish and hands flop without the slightest under-standing. Kumu Patrick's version is a parody of a parody, by dancers who can code-switch with their hips.

ALL IN THE FAMILY

In the old days, a hālau was carried on within a literal family; today it thrives through a figurative one—and a surprisingly inclusive one, at that. Nā Lei Hulu has plenty of gay students, one transgender one, and many more straight ones. There are mothers and daughters in the same class, brothers and sisters, husbands and wives. There is one three-generation family of dancers. And at practice on Sunday, mothers dance with their newborns in slings, toddlers sit on quilts and fiddle with iPads, and Kumu Patrick more than occasionally invites one to sit with him onstage, pointing out Mommy or Daddy in line.

Kumu Patrick and Casper

One of those daddies is Jason Laskey, a half-Japanese, half-Irish-English-German-French senior investment manager at Wells Fargo. Laskey met his wife, Lola, in the performing group, and their two young sons come to many rehearsals. Laskey joined the hālau in 2001 and says that Kumu Patrick's charisma is what has kept him coming back. "You just want to hear what he has to say," Laskey adds. "He's well read and articulate and finds ways to explain things to us."

As a way of explaining what distinguishes Kumu Patrick as a teacher, and the particular challenges of teaching after the diaspora, Laskey mentions a legendary peak on Oʻahu's windward coast that figures in "Pua ʻĀhihi," a dance inherited from Aunti Maiki. "Sixty or seventy percent of his students have never seen Lanihuli," Laskey points out, "but he finds a way to help them imagine the peak by regaling them with stories about it."

There are no soloists, per se, in the company, but among the men, Ryan Fuimaono is hard to miss. He's tall and half-Samoan and can't keep the smile off his face when he's on stage. After having performed at family gatherings, with a Polynesian revue as a child in San Diego, and then with various Bay Area groups, Fuimaono says he has found his place in Nā Lei Hulu. "I like how meticulous he is, in creating a vision but also in terms of our lines and spacing," says Fuimaono about Kumu Patrick. "He's a Virgo, I'm a Virgo," he adds, half-jokingly.

A social worker for the City of San Francisco, Fuimaono appreciates the structure of the hālau, which, he says, allows for expressive freedom. "It's comforting to be held by a group of people," he says, "to be able to tap into certain emotions and feel safe in the group." Like many members of the company, as well as the larger hālau, he mentions the sense of being part of a family. He grew up Samoan-style, with lots of siblings and cousins around, big family meetings, and a way of resolving family conflicts that reflected the chief system of the village back in Samoa. The sense of family merges with a sense of place and a feeling about that place: "I live in the Mission, we are based in San Francisco, and in dancing and chanting to honor San Francisco, we give back. It feels very Polynesian."

In fact, the Hawaiian concept of ʻohana—extended clan, chosen family, or important community—is a significant operating principle here. Classmates are "hula brothers and sisters." The dancer who teaches featherwork is Uncle Herman.

WHY I DANCE

People have often asked me why I dance hula when I'm not Hawaiian. I don't ever have the same answer. Some really tough sociopolitical-economic realities have driven Pacific Islanders like me to other places. When I was young, my Samoan identity was solidified by my upbringing: my close extended-family network, the importance of song and dance that was instilled in us kids, the foods we ate. But as an adult I've had to find ways to culti-vate my islander-ness. I dance because it's what I've always done. I dance because I love the physicality of a regular dance class. I dance because I love the commu-nity it creates.

But I also dance as a spiritual and political practice—spiritual because we honor the gods and goddesses of ancient Hawai'i, and in doing so we honor the ancient wisdom of all Hawaiians, Samoans, Tongans, and also Native Americans. All indigenous people knew that man and nature are interconnected. So in hālau, when we dance a show and wear lei and then later take care not to just throw the lei away but to return it to the earth, we are honoring that ancient knowledge. Because Kumu is passing down this knowledge, we have a space to do these very islander things in this very modern America.

And it's political because when we honor Hawai'i's royalty, when we invoke the true and ancient names of the land, the winds, the seas, we are resisting assimilation. We are saying, *We remember! We won't forget about this!* This remembering gives life to the sovereignty movement and gives purpose to us islanders who can feel displaced. This remembering builds our mana, our power.

—Ryan Fuimaono

Kumu Patrick thanks Aunty Bobbie

Barbara "Aunty Bobbie" Mendes sits at a table in the back of the hall for every class, in a striking red-and-gold skirt. She collects the money, scolds you if you get out of line, and jumps up to join her favorite dances, especially the oldies. A combination of strong aunt, wise elder, and bookkeeper, she is an indispensable part of the functioning of the hālau.

This is, after all, extended family as arts organization. But even in a smaller and more old-school hālau, various members take on other prescribed roles to help the group. These positions were once called *kōkua* and today are called "social media manager," "grantwriter," and "costume designer."

The traditions of hula demand respect for all elders, and certainly for the kumu. This translates into both loyalty and fealty to a sometimes arcane set of rules and behaviors that have been passed down for generations. Called "protocol," these rules range from taking off your shoes as you enter class and greeting fellow students never with a handshake, always with a kiss, to trusting in a kumu's every decision.

There can be an odd side to such traditions—and to belonging to a new family, even if a chosen one. Affection for the kumu can border on slavishness. Group dynamics can get dicey. Psychologists might note rampant projection. The ability to manage the expectations of 350 students is part of the job description of any kumu. But not all kumu are able to exhibit not just the "charisma" that Jason Laskey notes, but a kind of persuasiveness that would be called "leadership" in the MBA world. Kumu Patrick seems to have a special ability to find hidden talents in his motley group of students and former students—among them multimedia designers from Apple, former secretaries with wicked organizational skills, and business owners able to whip together a fund-raiser—and then convince them to become highly effective volunteers.

"Nā Lei Hulu hits all the marks of a healthy arts organization," says Lily Kharrazi, a dance ethnographer with Alliance for California Traditional Arts (ACTA), a nonprofit that provides services to traditional artists. "For thirty years, he has produced an annual season, maintained an audience, sold out the Palace of Fine Arts Theatre, engaged multiple communities and multiple ages, and successfully applied for grants. People in the arts world salivate over the kind of donor base he's developed."

Kharrazi notes that there are some qualities particular to hālau that make Kumu Patrick's task easier: "There is a group consciousness in hula, so group effort is taken to an extent that would be the envy of other arts organizations. It's values-based—respect, the idea of communal sharing, and loyalty to the kumu are paramount. But even for a hālau, Nā Lei Hulu is unusual."

For his part, Kumu Patrick credits San Francisco for his hālau's longevity. "We've been able to grow and be successful *in California*," he notes, with a tad of incredulity. "It is an irony that hula not in Hawai'i gets so much more of a lift, in terms of grants and organizational support, than hula in Hawai'i. The San Francisco environment, with its love of ethnic dance, has actually helped us grow our culture."

STAYING TETHERED

Kumu Patrick has learned a lot about himself over the past thirty years. One thing that's been an issue from the beginning—a common one for creative types—is how to blend his personal and his professional life. All his romantic partners have had to learn to "live with my mistress, which is hula," he says, laughing. "I tell them at the beginning, 'We're in a canoe. You have to either pick up this paddle and help or get off.'"

Bob Davis was his first partner in San Francisco, and his way of paddling was to give Kumu Patrick critical feedback. In fact, Davis is largely responsible for the talk-story format Kumu uses in his shows. "He told me he didn't feel included when he watched my early shows," Kumu Patrick explains. "He wanted much more context, so I developed that format to bring the audience in."

Since 2010, Kumu has been in a relationship with Rob Edwards, a real estate agent and former city planner. They share a loft apartment in Dogpatch, under the freeway, heavy on the black décor, the Apple devices, and the coconut water in the fridge. Occasionally an orchid graces the long table in the kitchen area. And then there is the tongue-in-cheek kuahu, or altar, made of giant rubber Incredible Hulk hands always hung with dried lei.

Edwards is a fixture at Kumu's shows, helping set up and break down dressing rooms, delivering flowers, and watching dress rehearsals. He often acts as a sounding board as well. "My students can't tell me that something doesn't work," Kumu Patrick says. "I need a Michelle Obama—someone who can say, 'What was *that*?'" He lets out a long, hearty laugh. Then he shares Edwards's perspective on his role as a kumu: "Rob says he has never witnessed someone vacillate so wildly between unparalleled generosity and unbridled tyranny."

Of course, Kumu Patrick also has sounding boards with whom he is not romantically involved. "Julie Mau has been with me since 1990," he says. Mau is the general manager of the hālau, a San Francisco firefighter, and a daughter of Wai'anae, on the rough leeward coast of O'ahu. "She brings that Hawaiian local perspective," he says. "And this hālau could not function without Julie."

But his closest creative partner, emotional supporter, performance soloist, and sometime muse is his own hula sister Shawna Alapa'i. The two danced with The Brothers Cazimero, moved from Hawai'i to the Bay Area, founded their respective hālau, and later traveled together to Hawai'i for 'ūniki training with Aunti Mae.

"Pua ʻĀhihi"

"Firemen's Hula," featuring Julie Mau (center)

"You need a peer to bounce things off of. She is the yin to my yang," he says, using the Chinese metaphor but then returning to the Hawaiian notion of duality, of ever-present male and female principles. Then he chucks the language of philosophy: "I can make prettier lei than she can, and she can kick my butt paddling a canoe."

As time goes on, Kumu Patrick has begun to step back and allow new collaborators to step up. After all, his once-jet-black hair is now steely gray and he is preparing for a second hip surgery. Now that he is fifty-five, some realities are hitting home. "I have a different level of energy," he says. "But it causes me to be more present. I don't want to miss anything my students are going through. And it means that when I illustrate a move, they better take notice, 'cause I'm only doing it once!"

He began giving high-level training to twenty students in 2002. It took loads of work on their part—research, preparing for class, learning a new hula style—and dogged perseverance, but some of those students have taken on important roles. Debbie Garcia teaches in Kumu Patrick's absence and choreographs dances; John Shima and Debbie Tong play ipu and ʻukulele in class and adopt a behind-the-scenes role outside it. Makani da Silva and Julie Mau teach the keiki, or children's, classes.

"The Sunday group knows how to rehearse without me," Kumu Patrick says. "Now that Debbie and John are able to lead the other classes, I am freed up to be creative in new ways. I can prepare for Merrie Monarch. I can take my kumu hat off and put my student hat back on, taking classes again. I can go to LA to pick fabrics for the dresses for this next show.

"In the old days, I would only leave hula for a hula reason. Now I can call in sick. Or have a guilt-free vacation."

Kumu Hula Shawna Alapaʻi dances "Waikīkī," accompanied by Kūpaoa.

"Kaimana Hila"

It takes prodding, though, to get him to admit to nonhula diversions. "A good portion of my life outside hula is spent at the gym," he says. "Inside my body is a fat Hawaiian boy screaming to get out, so I keep going to the gym and only let him out on special occasions." But he does admit to taking time to see modern dance, ballet, and theater. In the spring of 2016, he was trying to score tickets to *Hamilton* in New York City.

He doesn't wear his bookishness on his T-shirt sleeve, but his love of a good read makes itself apparent in class, whether he is referring to scholarly tomes he goes back to again and again (like *Mai Paʻa i ka Leo*, by Puakea Nogelmeier) or pulling from the latest *Harry Potter* book (or movie). Ask him, and he'll tell you that his bookshelf contains *Zealot: The Life and Times of Jesus of Nazareth*, by the Iranian American writer Reza Aslan; A *Confederacy of Dunces*, by John Kennedy Toole; and what he calls his all-time-favorite book, *The Curious Incident of the Dog in the Night-Time*, a 2003 mystery by British writer Mark Haddon.

While Kumu Patrick tries to stay on top of mainland culture, he says it is even more important for him to stay bound to Hawaiʻi, to "the foundation." He goes back to the island as often as possible and brings Hawaiian kumu, scholars, musicians, and craftsmen to San Francisco to offer his students workshops and special programs. (The ethnomusicologist Amy K. Stillman notes that this penchant for collaboration is a hallmark of California hālau.)

In 2014, Kumu Patrick achieved a hālau first: he took a four-month sabbatical in Honolulu, returning to San Francisco just once a month to check on his classes. He gave himself a relatively light choreography load by staging, for his annual October show, a *hōʻike nui*, or "grand recital," featuring a total of two hundred

John Shima and Debbie Garcia

dancers from all but his most beginner class. (Members of the performing group were able to take a rest and play just a backstage role.)

In their heterodox totality, they gave a proud image of the hālau's diversity and size.

They danced kahiko; they danced 'auana. They danced sacred dances; they danced sassy dances. The aunties danced; the keiki danced. And even the kumu danced.

At the end of the first half, a collection of men from different classes danced "Noho Paipai," the rocking-chair hula. (See page 12.) *Kāne* (men) are usually scattered throughout different classes, vastly outnumbered by women. "It was an unusual chance to dance together, just kāne," says one of them, Daniel "Pono" Sternbergh, who speaks Hawaiian and sprinkles his sentences with Hawaiian words, including the name of Kū, the Hawaiian equivalent of the Roman Mars or the Greek Ares. "Kumu surprised us all by jumping in. What a privilege! Very few kumu dance with their students. There was such Kū energy—a real 'man' moment."

"I Left My Heart in San Francisco," Union Square

CHAPTER EIGHT

Hit & Run Hula

You are walking through a BART station, underground in San Francisco. From a boom box somewhere, a capella voices are singing in harmonies that sound faintly Hawaiian. You head toward the automated machine to add value to your ticket. Then, out of the corner of your eye, you see a tall, pregnant woman in a coral-and-red-striped dress and pink tennies, black hair flowing down her back. She has walked to the center of a circular design in the concrete floor and has started to dance. You fill your ticket and walk toward the electronic turnstile.

Wait. Two more women, in tight capris and sandals, have joined her in the center of the circle. They are dancing, too, in precise coordination with the woman in the pink tennies.

You stop and reverse direction, away from the turnstile. Now there's a guy dancing behind them in a red T-shirt and running shoes. And another—real tall, big smile—in a tie-dyed shirt. Then another and another and another. Soon there are two dozen, all dancing in four neat lines.

"Hualalai" in the Apple Store, San Francisco

"Hualālai" in the Powell Street BART station, San Francisco

"When the guy with the red T-shirt started walking toward the women, I thought, 'Uh-oh,'" one observer later notes. His fears of a confrontation soon evaporated. "They all blended in with one another so well! And the men were as graceful as the women but still manlike."

The song, it turns out, is "Hualālai," from the Hawaiian vocal group Nā Palapalai. The dancers are from Nā Lei Hulu i ka Wēkiu.

This is but one of ten instances of flash-mob hula that Bay Area pedestrians witnessed one day in August 2009—in Union Square, at Dolores Park, in an Apple Store, in Golden Gate Park, at the Ferry Building, and at the Academy of Sciences. The dancers didn't stop until they'd kicked up sand at Ocean Beach. Their *Hit & Run Hula* numbers were accompanied by music not just from Nā Palapalai but also from Tony Bennett, M.C. Hammer, and Lady Gaga. In the Castro, they added a drag queen to the mix.

Then they took *Hit & Run Hula* to New York's Times Square. They even performed at thirty-eight thousand feet, in the aisles of a jumbo jet bound for Honolulu.

The idea for *Hit & Run Hula* sprouted in 2008, when the San Francisco arts organization Dancers' Group approached Kumu Patrick to present dance outside of a typical theater setting. Having successfully expanded notions of what hula might be, the unconventional kumu was ready to expand notions of who might see it. That's when he came up with the idea of hula, guerrilla style. He would catch the audience off-guard—on buses and airplanes, cable cars, and BART trains—and add a twist to something familiar.

In the theater, he has done this with hula mua, his mash-up of traditional hula movements with modern, non-Hawaiian music. But *Hit & Run Hula* takes Hawaiian dance completely out of context. "He likes to break people's preconceptions of hula and shake things up—the package, the form, the way it's experienced," says dancer and hālau business manager Julie Mau.

Wayne Hazzard, executive director of Dancers' Group, calls the viewers an "accidental audience": passersby, tourists, people on errands, joggers, and others who don't expect it will be hit with an energetic and mirthful hula troupe. "How fun to see a group of dancers out of the blue," he says, "across the street or off in the distance on a hillside."

"Our hālau thrives on zany adventures," Kumu Patrick says simply.

Some of Kumu Patrick's signature stage pieces stretch the politics of his hula even further than the flashmob stuff. One of them, "Hula's Bar & Lei Stand," takes as its departure point a place Kumu Patrick calls a "cultural landmark" more significant than "the state capitol or the Bishop Museum."

"Built in 1974," he tells his audiences, "Hula's Bar & Lei Stand ushered in the disco era to a ripe-and-ready population in Honolulu." True to its name, the venerable gay bar had a refrigerated lei stand in the front entrance. To the right were the bar and dance floor, to the left an outdoor patio where patrons cavorted in the balmy Hawaiian night. And smack in the middle, grounding the entire establishment, was a huge banyan tree, its horizontal branches creating an awning over both patio and bar. "It was covered with thousands of Christmas lights, giving you island-trash festiveness throughout the year," Kumu Patrick adds.

There was freedom at Hula's, not just to a kumu in the making but also to freshly minted adults like this author, who in 1975 had just turned eighteen and was eager to follow friends to Hula's and try on new identities out of her parents' sight.

"History Repeating" in the Castro district, featuring Matthew Martin

"He Inoa no Aunty Genoa Keawe Pāpālina Disco Megamix"

"Although it was known as a gay club," Kumu Patrick says, "Hula's always catered to a mixed crowd. It was a sanctuary, a disco, a favorite hangout—a place where you could be comfortable in a kimono, a tuxedo, or shorts and slippers.

"It was also a haunt for local celebrities and the place to go to see visiting movie stars and pop icons, such as Dolly Parton, Rudolph Nureyev, Elton John, Dorothy Lamour, and the best damn Diana Ross impostor I've ever seen. There was no VIP section. Dolly had to sit down next to Joe Blow from Kāneʻohe, wearing his surfer shorts and puka shell necklace, or Ronnie Boy Pacheco as Diana Ross." (In 1998, Hula's closed its doors, on the corner of Kūhiō and Kalaimoku, to make way for a shopping center. But, like a tropical phoenix, it resurfaced across from the Honolulu Zoo in the Waikīkī Grand Hotel and just celebrated its forty-first anniversary.)

For performances at San Francisco's Palace of Fine Arts Theatre, designer Marty McGee manages to re-create the trunk, boughs, and Christmas lights of the giant Honolulu banyan. And Malia King, the costume designer, transports characters from the 1970s—with a little help from the dancers themselves, always ready for a bit of San Francisco–style Halloween. There are girls in halter tops, guys in lavalava, striped bell-bottoms, peace signs, lots of aloha shirts, and the flower-print bathing trunks islanders call "jams." Blossoms are tucked in the usual and not-so-usual places. One man wears a platinum blond wig, another Ray-Bans, and a woman in Rastafarian colors sports the most gigantic Afro ever witnessed on a San Francisco stage.

The music includes a frenetic disco megamix that scratches from Gloria Gaynor's "I Will Survive" to a hula classic whose title translates to "Your Sweet Cheeks" to Donna Summer. Then the crowd settles down, the lights go blue, and a special guest in silver lamé, knobby knees, and high heels takes the spotlight. This is

Matthew Martin in "History Repeating"

Matthew Martin, a drag performer, actor, and San Francisco hotshot known for his impersonation of Bette Davis. The singer here is Shirley Bassey, the big, brassy voice from James Bond soundtracks. The Hula's crowd dances backup. Suddenly, we've left Honolulu for Hollywood gone haywire, or very bad Broadway, or maybe just *Beach Blanket Babylon*.

HULA AS SATIRE

Some of Kumu Patrick's recent dances aren't just hilariously funny valentines to places in his past, or outright spoofs, but seriously transgressive stuff intended as commentary on the way in which what he calls "an occupying culture" has seen hula.

Many Nā Lei Hulu shows include one dance or another that pokes fun at persistent stereotypes of hula, most of which have nothing to do with either the ancient art form or the modern ethnic dance. These faux images were formed over a half century: "Hula girl" impresarios of the early twentieth century promoted the "naughty hula hula," Hollywood etched images of "Sweet Leilani" into our brains, and the tourist industry dished up silly songs with English lyrics. Even the toy industry furthered the idea that hula was little more than a lot of hip action: in the late 1950s, Wham-O started a Hula-Hoop craze, selling more than one hundred million plastic hoops in two years. (To this day, for a surprising number of the uninitiated, the slightest mention of the Hawaiian art form will elicit a faint smile, a faraway look, and reminiscences of childhood hours spent furiously moving the hips in circles.)

HULA GIRLS

In her 2011 book, *Aloha America*, the historian and ethnic studies professor Adria Imada explores dimensions of what she variously refers to as "hula girls," "hularinas," and "hula queens." In the early twentieth century, she writes, the notion of the "hula girl" emerged quickly and held fast. On circuits across the continental United States, Hawaiian women (some of whom, like Jennie "Kini" Wilson, had been dancers in Kalākaua's court) became ambassadors of aloha for the territory of Hawai'i. Performing in Hawaiian showrooms in New York City, Chicago, and other metropolitan areas, they were often heralded as celebrities and success stories.

The hula girls were unwitting participants in a process that portrayed the peaceful colonization, Imada writes, of a territory that was not overly foreign or even dangerous. Hawai'i was presented, and then perceived, she adds, as "an eroticized and feminized space, a space disposed to political, military, and tourist penetration." Hula helped create an image of the islands as a safe sanctuary in which Hawaiians freely gave aloha and Americans eagerly accepted the hospitality.

The commercial performances by hula girls produced what Imada calls "an imagined intimacy between Hawai'i and the United States, enabling American audiences to experience a fantasy of Hawai'i as a different but welcoming place." Later, the luau (an Anglicization of the Hawaiian word *lū'au*, which actually refers to the tender leaf tops of the taro plant, a key ingredient in feasts) emerged at world's fairs in the United States. Luaus gained traction during World War II, when volunteer hula troupes staged luaus in the islands for arriving American soldiers, and then blossomed into the tourist luau. Luaus "helped to restabilize intimacy between Hawaiian colonial subjects and the military," Imada writes, and produced "an alchemy of rest and relaxation" for tourists.

These feasts (quite different from *aha'āina*, or traditional community feasts) evolved into today's very expensive, very cheesy, and very large gatherings of tourists at certain hotels, where entertainers are paid to sing and dance. Their dances may or may not be authentic, and often blur the lines between hula and the ethnic dances of, say, Tahiti and Samoa. But this is the image of hula that most Americans take home with them.

KINI "JENNIE" WILSON

One of the most famous hula girls of the early twentieth century was Ana Kini Kuululani McColgan, born in Honolulu in 1872 to a Hawaiian mother and an Irish tailor. She was adopted by a court dancer, Kapahukulaokamāmalu, and added that name to her own. When she was fourteen, King Kalākaua invited her to join the court's hula troupe, Hui Lei Mamo. She became one of seven dancers for the king and received training in Hawaiian and ballroom dance, as well as singing and 'ukelele. She is shown standing, third from left, below. Later known as Kini Kapahu, she toured the United States in 1893, performing in San Francisco; in Portland, Oregon; and at the World's Columbian Exposition in Chicago. The following year she toured Europe, performing in Paris at the Folies Bergère, in Germany for Kaiser Wilhelm II, and in Russia for Tsar Nicholas II. In 1909, she married engineer and, later, longtime Honolulu mayor John H. Wilson. The Hawai'i State Legislature designated "Aunt Jennie" Wilson, as she had become known, as honorary First Lady after the state was admitted to the union in 1959.

"Elements," with Hālau Nā Kamalei o Līlīlehua

"I want to take that stereotype and *own* it," Kumu Patrick says, his dark eyes bearing down on his lunch guest one sunny afternoon at Zut Tavern in Berkeley's Fourth Street district. "Me, a Native Hawaiian, turning it on its head and making it *cool*, making it better than it was."

He owns the stereotype for sure in "Gay Hawaiian Party," a dance named for the song that was recorded in 1964 and features twangy guitars and peppy singing by Alfred Apaka. The female Nā Lei Hulu members balance hilarious kitsch and subtle dancing. They present, with a wink and a lot of smiles, a light-hearted view of Hawaiian culture.

Other satirical numbers, like "Elements," are introduced with a fake-horrified riff on that standard of frat-party luaus: the grass skirt. Then come male dancers in tank tops and extravagant raffia skirts—more Village People than village Polynesians. Their athletic hula, danced to a remix of an underground house track by Danny Tenaglia, is syncopated, pulsating, and slightly creepy. See these dances once, and never again will you connect hula with Hula-Hoops.

Other hula don't skewer stereotypical images so much as co-opt them. Take Kumu Patrick's send-up of "The Hawaiian War Chant." As originally penned in the 1860s by Prince Leleiōhoku, the brother of Kalākaua, the song's title was "Kāua i ka Huahua'i" ("We Two in the Spray"). Its lyrics describe a clandestine meeting between two lovers. There was no "war" in the original, and the song was melodic, not a "chant." The original song was bastardized in 1936: Johnny Noble (the "king" of hapa-haole, or half-white, music) altered the tune, and new English lyrics were written. What had been a lovely, and authentic, Hawaiian song became a ridiculous ditty. Then "The Hawaiian War Chant" was recorded and popularized by everyone from the Muppets to

"TA-HU-WA-HU-WA-I"

the Michigan Marching Band. Check out YouTube, and you'll find it parodied by Spike Jones ("Auē," "hubba hubba hubba," weeping trombones, and Donald Duck–like quacks all make an appearance) and the Satin Dollz pinup dancers. ("Auē" becomes "oh-we," Carmen Miranda hairdos return, and the pinup dancers wreak havoc with Hula-Hoops.)

Kumu Patrick parodies the parody, or maybe deparodies it, turning the song into a medley that tells us a little bit about history, a little bit about the Hawaiian love of jazz, and a lot about the ability to take a joke and run with it. "If I Could Be with You (One Hour Tonight)/Ta-Hu-Wa-Hu-Wai" starts with women in clingy but elegant white dresses dancing, in a classic 'auana style, to a scratchy 1936 recording of "Hawaiian Hospitality" by Louis Armstrong, with Andy Iona and His Islanders. Then the 1940s sepia images fade away, replaced by a paisley pattern on the back scrim. The electronic music fades in over Armstrong's classic "If I Could Be with You"; it's a remix done by 46bliss. The women have mastered that "feminine mystique" mentioned in rehearsal—there are no sore necks in this balletic hula mua. Dancing in unison, their tight-fitting gowns flaring below the knee and swishing together, they call to mind a corps de ballet, minus the tutus and the anorexia.

The lights shift, and their lines become bands of an undulating rainbow. After a sassy little coda, their hips jutting and their hands hinging at the wrist, the girls are joined by the boys, who run onto the stage. We are back to the 1930s with a jazzy version of "The Hawaiian War Chant." The boys, in black, with white plumeria lei swinging, mix the Charleston with Popeye moves, their long limbs articulating like toy skeletons. The girls do the Satin Dollz one better, their hands flopping, their hips moving like pendulums, marking not

FROM SACRED TO PROFANE

[Nā Lei Hulu i ka Wēkiu is] showing how to bring traditional material into the present and the future. They have one of the truly great *corps de ballets* to be seen anywhere, and Patrick Makuakāne can use them polyphonically or in unison in a manner that challenges comparison with Doris Humphrey or Mark Morris, two of the most symphonic choreographers in the modern dance tradition. At one point in Saturday night's show, I found myself following three lines of counterpoint in the dance, and the thought flashed in my mind that Balanchine would have delighted in this.

Perhaps the most impressive choreography of the evening was an austere movement-choir piece about the missionaries that brought Doris Humphrey's great piece about the Shakers to mind—it had a similar architectural magnificence, relying on geometry, lines of force, contrapuntal intricacies, with some dancers verging on ecstatic possession, and others fighting with them—and set, with massive irreverence, to a disco beat....

Two hours of dancing in a variety of moods, from the sacred to the profane. It's wonderful to see a whole dance done kneeling down. The most wonderful thing of all is the way the movement seems to come from the dancers' hearts. The arms open up and reach with such strength and delicacy, and offer the dance to us with a generosity you have to see to believe. Their version of Roberta Flack's "The First Time Ever I Saw Your Face," with arms opening out to suggest "the moon and stars rose in your eyes," is alone worth the price of admission.

—Paul Parish, *Bay Area Reporter,* 2010

time but a hilarious understanding of how Hawaiian culture has been perverted. The dance chooses not to get polemic but rather to take the hilarity one step further, celebrating the full arc of Hawaiian history, rather than bemoaning it.

Kumu Patrick would be the last person ever to let academic buzzwords like "countercolonial" enter his onstage monologues. He is not afraid to make statements, though you might miss them in the effervescent mix of lights, music, action. One of his more political pieces, which he calls "Pig Dance," features the flying vagina of the hula goddess Kapo (making a feminist point, as well as being a bit in-your-face about uptight cultures). He considers political his willingness to talk about his gayness onstage, as well as his willingness to feature men in drag and women in power positions. His lifelong quest to convey the depth and diversity of Hawaiian culture is downright evangelistic, even if it's done with a smile, and in Hawaiian Creole.

"His artistry is that he can make a statement in a very light-handed way," says his "ex-ex" and lifelong friend Bob Davis. "He does a send-up, but it's with love. It's never mean-spirited. He's enjoying the joke in a very full, good-natured way."

HULA AS GLOBAL DERVISH DANCE

Some of this hula is revolutionary, sure, and it might even be "countercolonial." But some of it is just damn fun.

"Elements" comes pretty close to being like dancing in a club on a Saturday night. "Dangerous" comes dangerously close to tango. *Hit & Run Hula* was just a lot of hopping on buses, BART, and a Hawaiian Airlines jet.

"A lot of times, I go out there and I'm not trying to make a point," says Kumu Patrick. "I'm just playing around. And it works."

The innovations can be unsettling to his students and performers. Like the moment when he asked the women if they would dance topless in the opening to *Natives*. Like when he proposed *Hit & Run Hula*. Or like his most recent outlandish statement: "We are going to Burning Man."

If there were one dance that embodies that Nā Lei Hulu element of surprise—not to mention a bit of creative misbehavior—it might be "Krishna Hula," which is not so much hula as multiculti Carnaval. "Nothing I can say can convey the fizzy preposterousness of this piece," wrote Paul Parish, in the *Bay Area Reporter*, when "Krishna Hula" débuted at the Palace of Fine Arts Theatre. "I felt the building was going to explode."

Kumu Patrick loves to tell the story of its genesis. Here's how he did it at the performance of *Kanakolu* in 2015:

> "Every few years our beginning class has its first recital, or hōʻike, in Golden Gate Park. It's quite an affair, because, in addition to the performance, the dancers have to feed their invited guests. So that means bringing their costumes and lei, as well as teriyaki chicken, adobo, sushi, rice, *laulau*, poi, and all of that stuff. We usually meet at seven in the morning to set everything up.
>
> For one hōʻike, more than twenty years ago, it was a particularly hot Sunday afternoon. Whoo—so hot. The heat seemed to contribute to an electricity in the air. The general mood of everyone in the park was exuberant.

Sayali Goswami in "Krishna Hula," 2015

We were on a grassy area adjacent to the Rose Garden, on a mound overlooking JFK Drive and, beyond it, there was another grassy meadow, shaded by cherry blossoms and eucalyptus trees. [*He gestures with his strong arms to give his audience a sense of the topography.*] To the right, there is a huge cluster of trees blocking the view of the road as it meanders through the park.

I'm on my mound, I'm rehearsing the dancers, keeping the beat with my ipu and chanting (*Kahi mea i aloha*), and off in the distance, I hear a very faint sound—like chimes or little bells: *ching, ching ka ching ching, ching, ching ka ching ching, ching* . . . I'm wondering if I'm hearing things. I keep chanting (*Malama hewa 'ana 'oe, ahahana*), but the bell clanging gets louder and louder: *ching, ching ka ching ching, ching, ching ka ching ching, ching* . . ." And it's accompanied by its own chanting! *Hey-ah ching ching, hey-ah ching ching.* Pretty soon I feel that *my* chanting is actually accompanying the bell clanging, too.

Then, all of a sudden, out from behind the trees and into the road appears a parade of Krishna people. [*He raises his arms as though himself chanting and dancing with them.*] "Hare Krishna, Hare Krishna, Krishna, Krishna, Hare, Hare." We were like [*he slaps his hands together softly and chants demurely*], "*Ua pono no kau hana, ahahana,*" and they were like [*he raises his arms and belts it out*], "Krishna, Krishna, Hare, Hare," and we were, and they were, "Hare Krishna, hula Krishna, Hare Krishna, hula hula."

Finally, we just stopped to watch. They were having so much fun! They were magnificently dressed, jumping, clapping, singing, clanging, with wild abandon. It was a full-on celebration.

The funny thing was, no one was there to watch them but us. It's like they told people the wrong date of their parade. But it didn't matter. They seemed like they were in heaven.

If we had been in competition, Hindu people versus Hawai'i people, what would be the score? Definitely Krishna people: 1; hula dancers: 0.

Kumu Patrick didn't get mad—he got even. In 2002, he received a grant from the San Francisco Arts Commission to create a dance fantasy fusion of Hawaiian and East Indian influences. The result was "Krishna Hula," set to Boy George's "Bow Down Mister."

The curtain opens on a huge image of Radha, Krishna's eternal consort. She is young, nubile, wearing a yellow sari, her midriff bare and her neck encircled with flower garlands. In her left hand, she holds up a seashell.

A crowd of dancers vamp and swirl onto the stage, the women in saris and the men in dhotis. The dhotis are as white as pīkake (jasmine), but the saris are in a range of bright colors that recall the hues of a plumeria (or, as it's called in India, *champa*)—pinks, whites, yellows, reds. The dancers sit on the floor while a teacher in a black sari ascends a platform, with a bamboo rod, and points out the words to "Bow Down Mister." The "karma lesson" includes instructions like this, from the lyrics:

Do the right thing with your hands
Lay down on the painted sands
Whatever else your faith demands
Hare, hare, hare

"Krishna Hula"

The lesson continues blithely, with lines that sound variously lifted from a gospel song ("lift your hands up to the Lord"), from the Krishnas in Golden Gate Park ("Bow down mister/ Hare rama, hare Krishna"), or from the teacher in the corner yoga class ("Paint a *tilak* on your brow/ Open like a lotus now"). The dancers stand up and dance, with hula-like steps and arms thrown every which way in exuberant celebration.

Then the lyrics disappear, the screen behind them changes, and *kathak* ballerina Parna Basu darts onstage, the bells on her clothes whispering, her skirt swirling, her long braid flying. She is a sprite, a dervish, an inspiration. The Krishna-hula dancers skip, sway, jingle, and *namaste* in all directions around her. Basu's precise classical dance would make her a shoo-in for the most sophisticated Bollywood movie.

As the music morphs and transmogrifies, crazy associations occur to the viewer: Right—they have plumeria in India, too. Are those saris or muʻumuʻu? Is that a schoolteacher with a rod or an actress from a 1960s TV episode with "follow the bouncing ball"? Is that a kīhei over the dancer's shoulder, or a lost fragment of a sari? Would a Hindu god wear a lei? Is Boy George's "Bow Down Mister" a pseudo-Hindu song or his own version of "We Are the World"?

The piece ends with what have become almost iconic bits of choreography in the oeuvre of Kumu Patrick Makuakāne. First, the dancers form a circle around the kathak dancer, who is lifted onto the shoulders of a strong man. Many arms raise skyward, then bend in adulation of her. Then the dancers splay to both sides of the center platform, as Krishna—whose skin is painted cobalt blue and who wears a feathered turban— stands there and plays a flute. The choreography recalls "Salva Mea" (where the priest with the cross forms the apex), and *Daughters of Haumea* (where two lovers entwine on a sacred bed as the "women skilled in the art of lovemaking" encircle them), and "Hula Puaʻa" (or "Pig Dance," where swine surround a flower, a metaphor for Kapo's flying vagina).

Here, the dancers bow toward Krishna, then arch back, bow toward him and arch back. The kathak dancer takes a few last swirls, then rushes to the base of the platform and prostrates herself. The dancers bow toward Krishna, then arch back, bow toward him and arch back, their arms overhead, brushing through the air.

Is this adulation, or is it undulation, the graceful arms of Krishna devotees or the long tendrils of the sea anemone, waving over the ancient coral reef as the deepest waves wash through them—back, then forth, back, then forth?

Parna Basu in "Krishna Hula," 2008

"Manu ʻŌʻō" at the de Young Museum

Hōʻike Nui, 2009

Epilogue

When I was seven, my mother took me to the Waialua Gymnasium, a cavernous wood building near the sugar mill, for my first hula class. Until then, ballet had been my thing. But we'd just moved back to Hawai'i, where I was born, and the weather proved too sticky for tights and a leotard. My teacher was Mrs. Fanny Kuni, who was part of a church 'ohana whose patriarch was a preacher and whose members traveled the islands dancing and singing to raise funds. They were also known for their beautiful pageants and tableaux.

My memories from that Tuesday-night hula class are dim. One photo survives to help me: I am standing in a ti-leaf skirt and a yellow bikini top, holding a plumeria lei. It must have been taken moments before I put on the lei and went onstage.

The hula dances from that time that have stayed with me, though, are the ones I learned at Waialua Elementary School, where we had a big festival each year on May 1. There was even a maypole hula, performed by Mrs. Kauahikaua's fourth graders, although in Hawai'i May Day bears little resemblance to European rites. Instead, it is reimagined as Lei Day—a time when you honor friends and loved ones with fresh flower garlands.

Many schools hold pageants celebrating Hawaiian heritage, but ours was special. Hula dominated the program, but the different acts reflected the mix of races out in "the country," as we still call it. In addition to hula, schoolchildren performed a Chinese dragon dance, a Filipino *tinikling*, and a Samoan slap dance. The whole show started with a grand procession of the May Day Court: eight lucky sixth-graders were chosen as princesses of the eight Hawaiian islands, which meant each one wore elegant satin *holokū*—a flowing dress, usually with a train—in the color of her island, as well as lei made from the island flower. (I was always envious of the Princess of Kaua'i, in her violet dress and lei of *mokihana*.) Each princess was attended by a sixth-grade boy, who stood stiffly in a black suit and formal sash and carried a kāhili, or feathered staff. Then there was the May Day Queen, in white satin and long strands of crown flowers. She had to be a wonderful dancer, because her hula was the day's culminating event.

I loved each of the dances I learned at Waialua Elementary, especially the lullaby hula "Pūpū Hinuhinu" ("Shiny Shells") and the vigorous "Boy from Laupahoehoe." But, for various reasons, hula never felt like mine, or I somehow never felt part of *it*. This was made most painfully clear in fourth grade, when Mrs. Kauahikaua brushed and pinned the long black hair of my Native Hawaiian classmates while I stood nearby, ruing my blond curls.

My Honolulu high school, Punahou, lacked the multicultural flavor of the country. And there was a tacit understanding in those years that to participate in May Day, you had to be part Hawaiian. So I put my energy into modern dance and jazz and, later, Afro-Haitian and salsa. Then a knee injury in the mid-1980s made me stop dancing.

Several years after that, I happened to interview Patrick Makuakāne for a story and began to notice his troupe at the Hawaiian-music concerts that were becoming less infrequent in the San Francisco Bay Area. When I confessed to an older, Native Hawaiian friend that I was thinking about taking hula classes, she said, firmly, "If you're going to study the hula, you must study with Patrick." And so I did.

I joined the new "Thursday-night class." It still strikes me as odd: in San Francisco, in an elementary-school cafeteria very far from that of Waialua, hula has come to feel like mine, and I have come to feel a part of it. In the many years since, the ranks of that class and others have ebbed and flowed like the tide, as older dancers drop out, the class is combined with others, and the process repeats. After a job took me to the East Coast for three years, I dropped back to a less advanced class, which was recently combined with another. And so it goes in hālau. Sooner or later, you've danced with everyone, it seems. If you're lucky, you become an elder, maybe even joining the ranks of "the forever class," also known as "the gracious ladies."

Graciousness is but one of the things you gain over time with hula, as you try to embody the values your kumu teaches you. For hula is about much more than movement. I've tried to allude to some of those values here—respect, appreciation, pleasantness, patience, humility. But there are two that are especially noticeable to a student like me. One of them might be called "aloha," if that term weren't so misunderstood and overused. I prefer to think of it as loving-kindness. It has to do with the relationship you build with your kumu, a relationship that is predicated on mutual respect but also involves gentleness and generosity. The loving-kindness grows into something that is extended between and among hula brothers and sisters as well. It is especially meaningful in an urban world of virtual relationships, because it isn't very urban and it is not at all virtual. It is rooted in a certain place (a school cafeteria), at a certain day and time (Thursday, 7:00 P.M.), and with a certain group of people (hula brothers and sisters). But, of course, it also reaches backward to another place (Hawai'i) and other kumu (our lineage). And it reaches outward to students in other classes, and former students, and hālau helpers, and people who come to our shows, and other kumu and their students.

In 2008, the Wednesday class (now the senior class) participated in a *huaka'i*, or journey, to O'ahu. Here, they work in a *lo'i* (taro field).

Notes on Language and Glossary of Terms

The Polynesian tongue known as Hawaiian (or *ʻōlelo Hawaiʻi* within the language itself) has been the subject of much confusion and change over the past two centuries. It is the youngest language on the planet, but it is more complex than that fact may imply. Often the same word has multiple meanings that are not always related. And a tradition among native speakers of using kaona—metaphor or "hidden meaning"—in poetry, further complicates the easy definition of words. (See page 51 for an explanation of the poetic device.)

When Christian missionaries arrived in Hawaiʻi in 1820, the islands had no written language. In order to print a bible, they adapted the English alphabet and gave the written language twelve Latin letters, reducing many Hawaiian words to an overly simple spelling and pronunciation. (In fact, writers like Hiram Bingham quickly started adding certain diacritical marks to extend the alphabet.) After the 1957 publication of *The Hawaiian Dictionary,* by Mary Kawena Pukui and Samuel H. Elbert, spelling and diacritical marks in Hawaiian words were applied more consistently. The effort intensified after 1978, when ʻAhahui ʻŌlelo Hawaiʻi, a committee of Hawaiian-language teachers, met to standardize the entire scope of Hawaiian spelling.

Because of the few letters, two diacritical marks become essential in Hawaiian orthography, changing both the sound and the meaning of words in which they appear.

- **The 'okina** (the symbol ') is a unicameral letter in the otherwise-Latin Hawaiian alphabet. In English it is known as a glottal stop, as it precedes vowels and changes the way they are pronounced as well as the meaning. For example, the word *pau* (pronounced *pow*), spelled without any diacritical mark, means "finished," "ended," or "all done." But when spelled *pa'u* (*puh-oo*) with an 'okina, it gains a syllable and refers to "soot," "smudge," or "ink powder."

- **The *kahakō*** (the symbol ‾ over a vowel) indicates a vowel sound that is drawn out. In English, the symbol is known as a macron. Using the same three letters we just used, but adding an 'okina and a kahakō, we get *pa'ū* (*puh-oooh*), which means "moldy" or "moist." The word *pā'ū* (*pah-oooh*) means "skirt" and is used especially to refer to the long skirts worn by female equestrians, as well as the full skirts, gathered around the hips, used in hula practice.

In this book I have followed the style guidelines that I and a team of editors have evolved for *Kaholo'ana*, Nā Lei Hulu's annual newsletter. We italicize Hawaiian words on first reference only, but proper nouns—the names of people, places, songs, or hālau—get no italics at all. In cases where a Hawaiian word has become part of the English lexicon—like *kahuna* or *lei*—we do not italicize it if it appears in an English context, or if it appears unitalicized in quoted text. ("Each guest was presented with a lei," the newspaper reported.)

'Ōlelo Hawai'i also has a distinct system for marking plural nouns, using the article (or marker) *nā*, rather than a terminal *s*. Unless a word has been fully adopted in English and is being used in an English context or quote ("The hapa-haole song 'Leis for Sale' was written in 1934 by Johnny Noble"), we resist adding an *s* to indicate the plural form.

In cases where a Hawaiian word with diacriticals has been Anglicized or bastardized without them—like *luau*—we retain that spelling in a quote or a title, or when referring to tourist feasts, but use the 'olelo Hawai'i word—*lū'au*—if we are referring to the tender tops of taro leaves.

We do not put an 'okina in the English adjective *Hawaiian,* but we do use it in the place name *Hawai'i.*

When we are citing Hawaiian words used in books or other printed sources, we generally defer to the spelling and styling of the original printed text. Likewise, we try to defer to the preferences of authors and kumu hula on the spelling of their own names or the names of their hālau.

In describing the indigenous people of the Hawaiian archipelago, as well as their descendants, many Hawaiian activists and scholars now use *kanaka maoli* (*kanaka* means "people," and *maoli* refers to a native). We simply use "Native Hawaiians." To avoid confusion, we do not apply the word *Hawaiian* to everyone who lives in Hawai'i. (The term is not analogous to, say, *Californian* or *Floridian.*)

For translating individual Hawaiian words, we have used *The Hawaiian Dictionary* of Mary Kawena Pukui and Samuel H. Elbert, as well as Ulukau, the Hawaiian Electronic Library (www.wehewehe.org). This is an extension of the many-pronged efforts by educators and native speakers of Hawaiian to revitalize the language, an undertaking that has been ongoing since the 1980s and whose effects ripple through the world of hula.

The Hawaiian language continues to be better defined and understood with each decade. We have sought the advice and help of language speakers and professors in navigating its sometimes confusing waters, but any mistakes here are entirely ours.

"He Mele Hoʻi"

GLOSSARY OF TERMS

Among the many Hawaiian words that appear in this book, the following is a list of the ones that appear repeatedly and seem most important to students and aficionados of hula.

ʻai haʻa: hula plié; low, bent-knee stance

ʻāina: place; land

akua: god or goddess; also plural (gods or goddesses)

ao: day; light; the world of living people

ʻaumakua: family god; deified ancestor

auē: oh! alas! too bad!; sometimes spelled auwē

haʻa: ritual movements performed for gods at temples

haku mele: master of song

hālau: school of hula

hānai: fostered or adopted person, following the informal Hawaiian custom

hānau: born; to be born

haole: foreigner; white person; plural is haole

hapa haole: literally "half white," the term has come to refer to a genre of Hawaiian music and the dances that go along with it

heiau: temple; shrine

hīmeni: Hawaiian hymns

hōʻike: festival; recital (a hōʻike nui is a "grand recital")

hoʻopaʻa: chanter

hoʻopuka: dance or sequence of steps allowing the dancer to enter the stage area

hula ʻālaʻapapa: dance, accompanied by an ipu heke, that is performed outside of temple rituals; it evolved from pre–Western contact, and honors gods

hula ʻauana: literally "wandering hula"; the Western-influenced, modern hula

hula kahiko: traditional form of hula that is most closely linked to the ancient form

hula kuahu: sacred, ritualistic hula performed under protection of a hula divinity

hula kuʻi: dance of Kalākaua's era, combining old and new styles

hula maʻi: dance that celebrates procreation and encourages perpetuation of the family line

hula mua: "progressive" hula, pioneered by Kumu Hula Patrick Makuakāne, that sets traditional and modern styles of movement to nontraditional music

hula ʻōhelo: a sequence of movements in which a dancer reclines on the ground, leaning over to one side while supporting him- or herself with one hand, and makes sawing motions with the opposite foot and arm

hula ʻōlapa: like hula ʻālaʻapapa, hula accompanied by an ipu heke

hula pahu: especially sacred dance accompanied by a pahu drum

i mua: forward; onward

ipu: gourd drum

ipu heke: double-gourd drum

kāhili: feather standard or staff, symbolic of royalty

kāholo: hula's most basic step; the other basic steps include ʻami, ʻami kūkū, hela, kāʻō, kāwelu, lele, lele ʻuehe, ʻōniu, and ʻuehe

kahu: guardian; minister

kanakolu: thirty

kāne: man; plural is also kāne

kanikau: dirge; lament

kaona: purposely hidden meaning of a poetic piece; metaphor; double entendre

kapa: cloth made primarily from the pounded bark of the *wauke,* or paper mulberry tree

kapu: forbidden; sacred

keiki: child, children

kīhei: long, one-shoulder garment printed with symbols of a particular hula line; symbol of the authority of one who has gone through the ʻūniki process

kōkua: help; assistance; relief; supporter

kuahu: altar

kūʻauhau: pedigree; lineage; old traditions; genealogy; genealogist

kuleana: privilege; right; responsibility; calling

kumu: teacher; source of knowledge and tradition

kumulipo: slime; the deep darkness (time before humans)

kupuna: elders in the community

lehua: the flower from the ʻōhiʻa tree, sacred to Pele

lei hulu: a garland made of feathers

lei poʻo: a garland made of flowers or feathers, worn on the head

liko: tender bud; young, attractive man

lipo: deep blue-black, as a cavern, the sea, or a dense forest

lūʻau: the tender leaf tops of the *kalo*, or taro plant

luau: The Anglicized version of lūʻau, which has come to be the term referring to a touristy feast or party

māhū: gay; transgender

maile: prized, fragrant mountain vines used as adornment for hula dancers

malo: loincloth

mana: divine power

mele: poetic texts or chants; chants meant to be accompanied by dance; also a verb meaning to chant a mele

mele ʻāina, or mele aloha ʻāina: songs of the land; chants extolling important or familiar places

mele hoʻoipoipo: love chant

mele hula: chant for hula

mele inoa: name chant

mele maʻi: chants celebrating procreation

mele oli: chants not meant for dancing

moʻo: lizard; dragon; magic lizard-dragon

moʻokūʻauhau: geneology; origins

mua: either the past or the future; a while

niki: to tie

ʻohana: extended family

ʻōlapa: dancer or group of dancers

oli kāhea: chant asking permission to enter to receive knowledge

oli komo: welcoming chant granting permission to enter the place of instruction

pā: rhythmic refrain; movement pattern between verses of a chant

pahu: drum whose body is carved from the trunk of a tree, then stretched with either sharkskin or cowhide

pāʻū: skirt; hula practice skirt

pīkake: Arabian jasmine

piko: umbilical cord; also used for "center"

pō: night; darkness; the spirit world

poʻe hula: people of hula

pua: flower

pua līlīlehua: red sagebrush flower

puka: come forth; hole

pūniu: small knee drum

ti, tī, or kī: an evergreen flowering plant, cultivated throughout Polynesia, whose long and broad green leaves are used to make lei and hula skirts, to wrap and store food

ʻulīʻulī: feathered gourd rattler

ʻulu: breadfruit

ʻūniki: formal graduation ceremony; ancient practice used to elevate teachers

wahine: woman; the plural is wāhine

walewale: slime out of which all life emerges

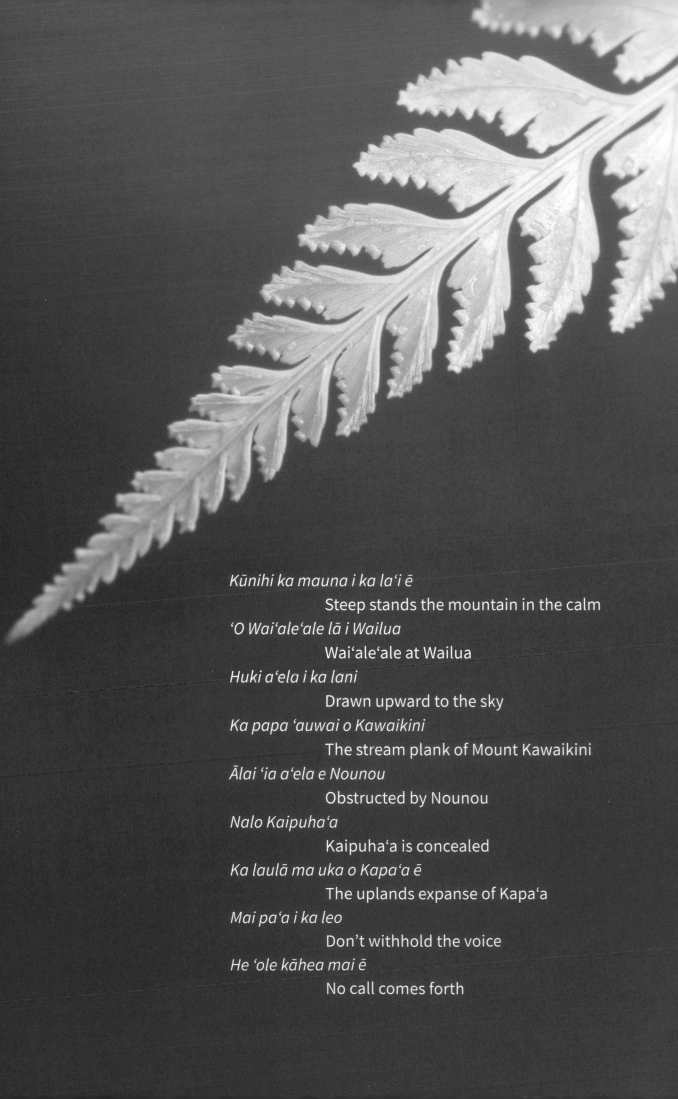

Kūnihi ka mauna i ka laʻi ē
    Steep stands the mountain in the calm
ʻO Waiʻaleʻale lā i Wailua
    Waiʻaleʻale at Wailua
Huki aʻela i ka lani
    Drawn upward to the sky
Ka papa ʻauwai o Kawaikini
    The stream plank of Mount Kawaikini
Ālai ʻia aʻela e Nounou
    Obstructed by Nounou
Nalo Kaipuhaʻa
    Kaipuhaʻa is concealed
Ka laulā ma uka o Kapaʻa ē
    The uplands expanse of Kapaʻa
Mai paʻa i ka leo
    Don't withhold the voice
He ʻole kāhea mai ē
    No call comes forth

Acknowledgments

"Kūnihi ka Mauna" is a *mele kāhea*, an "entrance chant," that Kumu Patrick Makuakāne teaches his intermediate and advanced classes. Students use it to ask permission to enter the classroom and receive knowledge. (It might be used in other moments to beg permission to enter a home, the forest, a museum, or any other place housing a distinguished elder.)

The mele is set on the island of Kaua'i, where "steep stands the mountain Wai'ale'ale in the calm." According to the historian Nathaniel Emerson, the chant comes from the story of Hi'iaka, when Pele's sister journeys to fetch Chief Lohi'au. She and her entourage come by a steep and narrow path to the brink of the Wailua River, which should have been spanned by a single plank. But the bridge was removed by an ill-tempered mo'o named Wailua, like the stream. Hi'iaka calls out, demanding that the plank be restored to its place. Wailua does not recognize Hi'iaka and makes no response. At this, the goddess summons all her strength, and Wailua, outmatched in power and reduced to her true station as a mere reptile, seeks refuge in the caverns beneath the river. Hi'iaka then makes the crossing better for others by laying down stepping-stones, which remain to this day.

For today's chanter, the goal in giving voice to this chant is attaining *'ike* ("knowledge") from a kumu, recognizing that the path will be as challenging as that of Hi'iaka. From below, at Kapa'a, along the Wailua River, we behold the summit. But between it and us sits the hill Nounou (now called the Sleeping Giant) and, hidden from view, the broad plain of Kaipuha'a ("the gourd of humility"). Reaching the summit of Kawaikini requires traversing both these terrains. In other words, the steep path to knowledge requires respecting the challenges before us, and it leads straight through humility.

I have appealed to many to help me on the daunting journey of making this book. Some people I have asked quite directly. Others I have asked by reading their work or listening to their words or watching their movements, trying to open myself up to the beauty they offer. Many answered my call, and I am humbled and honored by what they shared. I hope I have done them justice.

I would like to express my gratitude first to the writers and scholars whose works are cited within the text. Dr. Keanu Sai helped me see Hawai'i's nineteenth-century story in a new light. Lucia Tarallo Jensen gave me a window into life in Hawai'i several centuries ago. Rita Ariyoshi did a lot of gumshoe work on Aunti Maiki, though "gumshoe" is a strange term to use when you are referring to subjects most often found barefoot. Benton Sen gave insight on Robert Cazimero and the ancient story of hula. Especially inspiring were Jerry Hopkins, for his 1982 volume, *The Hula*, and Amy K. Stillman, for her 2011 update of it. Stillman's *Sacred Hula: The Historical Hula 'Ala'apapa*, though, blew open my own understanding of hula kahiko especially.

In fact, those books are just two of many works by Stillman that have proved invaluable to me. But to thank her just for her books misses the mark. In the many conversations I have had with her over many years, she has been unfailingly patient, perspicacious, and gracious. Her students at the University of Michigan and elsewhere are lucky to have her.

Another scholar who has helped on this and many related projects is Puakea Nogelmeier. How someone wears so many different hats and yet still picks up his phone every morning at a certain hour, to answer what must seem like elementary questions, is a testament not just to his time management skills but also to his deep generosity and his desire to make sure a reporter gets her story straight.

Each of my kumu's kumu also heard my call, let me in, and shared his or her *mana'o*: John Keola Lake in 2004, Robert Uluwehi Cazimero and Mae Kamāmalu Klein in 2015.

Mahalo ā nui—great gratitude.

Within the hālau, key people have truly made this book possible. I must thank the newsletter crew—Jenny Des Jarlais, Chris Lauer, Linda Zane, Kailani Moran, Julie Mau, and Edna Cabcabin Moran. For fifteen years they have helped put out a newsletter that always contains little pearls, lively articles, exuberant photos, and luscious graphics. Many of the chapters of this book started as articles in the newsletter, and I am ever so thankful to them for their high standards, artistry, and verve.

Two of those in the newsletter crew deserve special mention. The deputy editor, Jenny Des Jarlais, read several chapters in early drafts and gave terrific suggestions. She took over the management of the 2016 newsletter so that I could complete the manuscript. She contributed a sidebar. And she set aside a lot of competing duties as a professional editor, wife, and mother to read the final draft of the book, offering her unfailingly astute insights in the process. A surfeit of thanks goes to her.

Kailani Moran helped with the book in all kinds of unseen ways—fact-checking statistics, drafting sidebars, finding obscure texts, and becoming a mini-expert in hula pahu. But, as my research assistant over the past several years, she also started building my bibliography when the book was just a figment of my imagination, she helped put together the proposal, and she kept other fires in my professional life burning while I concentrated on the intricacies of hula. I owe her a great debt.

Once my words became a "manuscript," I was blessed with some true editorial talent. Jessie Scanlon read early chapters. Nan Wiener's incessant questions deepened the ideas, and her scalpel brought clarity to each chapter. Her enthusiasm for the story itself, and for dance, was invaluable. A book like this is a bear to copy-edit, but two rather amazing talents rose to the challenge: Julie Holland scoured the manuscript for Hawaiian words and checked them in dictionaries, online resources, and random Web sites. Annie Tucker attacked the sentences, bringing them grace. She found a frightening number of dangling participles, and she also indulged me on the spelling of "OK," the use and misuse of accent marks, and the applications of the passive voice.

How is it possible to translate to the page what Nā Lei Hulu does on the stage? How can you be true to an ancient art form while making it look hot and high tech? We threw down the gauntlet. Designer Tabitha Lahr picked it up. And then she surprised and delighted us.

Holding all of these last efforts together, and getting the book to the printer and the binder, was Brooke Warner. She was steady and strong, and she guided us through the bookmaking process, bringing impressive savvy to a project that was done outside the traditional bounds of publishing.

This book would not exist without the stunning photos of Julie Mau and, especially, Lin Cariffe. Thank you for your vision and your ability to put ineffable magic into pixels.

Julie Mau is also the general manager of Nā Lei Hulu i ka Wēkiu. She gave us unwavering support. Janie Revelo, Nicholas Tice, and Barbara "Aunty Bobbie" Mendes provided the infrastructure to allow us to independently publish. Aunty Bobbie is a pilar of the hālau, and her excitement about this book has been wind in the sail of our outrigger canoe. Charly Zukow and his team, especially James Smith, helped us spread the news about this book, bringing not just their professionalism but their enthusiasm. Leslie Rossman and Emily Terry believed in the book's national appeal and took us onto the airwaves.

Mahalo palena ʻole—gratitude without boundaries.

Some very personal relationships complemented these professional ones. My mother took me to my first hula class with Mrs. Kuni and has always been a willing escort to hula festivals. She has for years contributed to Nā Lei Hulu, but this year she gave us the ultimate support: she printed out and read the entire manuscript, applying both her deft sense of Hawaiian culture and her intimate familiarity with English grammar.

My husband, Bruce Lowell Bigelow, has watched many a night as I've come home after hula class and run through all the verses I've just learned. He's agreed to eat alone two or three times a week when I'm off dancing. And he's driven me to more shows than he might have imagined when he met me more than two decades ago. In thanks, I want to remind him that it is his voice and his arms I imagine every time I dance "Ke Aloha."

And then there is Kumu Patrick, who had the audacity to say, "Let's write a book," the patience to answer my every question, and the discretion to know when to step in and help and when to step back and let me have my say. He offers a guiding light for me and for many. He hears our voices. The ultimate thanks go to him.

Mahalo palena ʻole, mau a mau—gratitude without boundaries, forever.

Bibliography

The main print and online sources used for this book are listed below. In addition, a number of scholars and kumu hula—especially Robert Cazimero, Mae Kamāmalu Klein, Puakea Nogelmeier, and Amy Kuʻuleialoha Stillman—gave generously of their time and manaʻo, in interviews conducted in person and via e-mail.

The contributions of many of Kumu Patrick Makuakāne's friends, colleagues, and students are also reflected throughout the book. These include interviews with Makani da Silva, Bob Davis, Patty Ann Farrell, Ryan Fuimaono, Debbie Garcia, Lucia Tarallo Jensen, Kuana Torres Kahele, Lily Kharazzi, Jason Laskey, Julie Mau, Marty McGee, and Debbie Tong.

For students of the hula, or for scholars and journalists interested in digging more deeply into the literature, I recommend a visit to the ever-evolving blog of professor and kumu hula Amy Kuʻuleialoha Stillman. It contains a comprehensive bibliography of print sources, songbooks, and mele lyrics, as well as dissertations and theses: https://amykstillman.wordpress.com.

Adams, Wanda A. "Halau Presents Pleasing, Contemporary Take on Hula." *Honolulu Star-Advertiser*, May 11, 2014.

Aeto, John. "A Hula Legacy: Aunty Aggie and Kamaki Kanahele Share Stories of Their Hula Genealogy." *Mana*, November/December 2012.

Ariyoshi, Rita. *Hula Is Life: The Story of Hālau Hula O Maiki.* Honolulu: Maiki Aiu Building Corporation, 1998.

"The Background: Hawaiian Language Newspapers—a Timeline of Progress." Honolulu: Awaiaulu: Hawaiian Literature Project, 2012. Web. http://www.awaiaulu.org/main/index.php?option=com_content&view=article&id=58&Itemid=74.

Beckwith, Martha Warren, ed. *The Kumulipo: A Hawaiian Creation Chant.* Honolulu: University of Hawai'i Press, 1951.

Berger, John. "'Natives' Is Powerful Hula." *Honolulu Star-Bulletin*, March 27, 2001.

Cal Performances. "Study Guide: Nā Lei Hulu i ka Wēkiu." *SchoolTime*, 2006.

Charlot, John. "The Hula in Hawaiian Life and Thought." *Honolulu* magazine, November 1979.

Chong-Stannard, Joy, Craig Howes, and Victoria Nalani Kneubuhl, producers. *Maiki Aiu Lake.* Honolulu: Hawaii Public Television and the Center for Biographical Research of the University of Hawai'i–Mānoa, 2002.

Cook, Lynn. "Creative Callings: Native Arts Foundation Names Its 2014 Fellows." *Ka Wai Ola*, May 2014.

de Silva, Kihei. "Those Darned Traditionalists." Web. https://apps.ksbe.edu/kaiwakiloumoku/kaleinamanu/essays/those_darned_traditionalists.

Dunning, Jennifer. "Hawaiian-Style Lilt and Flow, with a Jab at Grass Skirts." *New York Times*, August 13, 2007.

Emerson, Nathaniel. *Unwritten Literature of Hawaii: The Sacred Songs of the Hula.* Honolulu: Mutual Publishing Company, 2007.

Enomoto, Catherine Kekoa. "Hula Family Tree." *Honolulu Star-Bulletin*, April 8, 1996.

Fournier, Rasa. "Newspaper Hula." *Midweek*, May 7, 2014.

Hale, Constance. Conversation with Mark Keali'i Ho'omalu, Lily Kharazzi, Patrick Makuakāne, Amy Ku'ulcialoha Stillman, and Michael Yamashita. San Francisco, June 5, 2010.

Hale, Constance. Interview with Patrick Makuakāne. San Francisco, multiple dates, beginning in 1990.

Hale, Constance. "The Hula Movement," *Atlantic*, July/August 2002.

Harada, Wayne. "Makuakane a Master of Hula Innovation," *Honolulu Star-Advertiser*, May 12, 2014.

Hawai'i Digital Newspaper Project/National Digital Newspaper Project. University of Hawai'i–Mānoa, 2013. Web. https://sites.google.com/a/hawaii.edu/ndnp-hawaii.

Hopkins, Jerry. *The Hula.* Honolulu: Bess Press, Inc., 2011.

Halau o Kekuhi. *Holo Mai Pele.* Pacific Islanders in Communications, 2001.

Hula: Hawaiian Proverbs & Inspirational Quotes Celebrating Hula in Hawai'i. Honolulu: Mutual Publishing, 2003.

"Ike Kū'oko'a: Liberating Knowledge." Honolulu: Awaiaulu: Hawaiian Literature Project, 2012. Web. http://www.awaiaulu.org/main/index.php?option=com_content&view=article&id=16&Itemid=41.

Imada, Adria L. *Aloha America: Hula Circuits through the U.S. Empire.* Durham, NC: Duke University Press, 2012.

Itagaki, Han M., and Lovina Lependu, eds. *Nānā I Na Loea Hula: Look to the Hula Resources: Volume II.* Honolulu: Kalihi-Palāma Culture & Arts Society, Inc., 1997.

Jensen, Lucia Tarallo. *Daughters of Haumea: Women of Ancient Hawai'i.* Honolulu: Pueo Press, 2006.

Kaeppler, Adrienne L. *Hula Pahu: Hawaiian Drum Dances, Vol. 1: Ha'a and Hula Pahu: Sacred Movements. Bishop Museum Bulletin in Anthropology* 3. Honolulu: Bishop Museum Press, 1993.

Kamae, Eddie and Myrna, directors. *Keepers of the Flame: The Cultural Legacy of Three Hawaiian Women.* Honolulu: The Hawaiian Legacy Foundation, 2005.

Kanahele, George S. and John Berger, ed. *Hawaiian Music and Musicians: An Encyclopedic History.* Honolulu: Mutual Publishing, 2012.

"Leina'ala ''Ala' Rebecca Kalama Heine." *Honolulu Star-Advertiser*, September 27, 2015.

Looseleaf, Victoria. "Hula Groups Sway to Kitschy Breezes." *Los Angeles Times*, August 5, 2002.

Makuakāne, Patrick. Interview with Robert Cazimero. San Francisco, April 4, 2014.

Musiker, Cy. "Hula from the Past, Advancing into the Future," KQED Arts, October 15, 2015. Web. http://ww2.kqed.org/arts/category/dance.

Nā Mamo Noʻeau. "Our Mission." Web. http://www.namamonocau.net/nav-us-our-mission.html.

"Nūpepa ʻŌlelo Hawaiʻi." *Hawaii Alive.* Bishop Museum. Web. 2011. http://www.hawaiialive.org/topics.php?sub=Unification+and+Monarchy&Subtopic=126.

Nogelmeier, Puakea. "Maiki Aiu Lake: Kumu Hula and Preserver of Hawaiian Culture." Study guide from *Biography Hawaiʻi: Five Lives.* Hawaiʻi Public Television and the Center for Biographical Research of the University of Hawaiʻi–Mānoa. Web. http://www.hawaii.edu/biograph/pdf/maikiguide.pdf.

Nogelmeier, Puakea. *I Ulu i ke Kumu: The Hawaiʻinuiākea Monograph.* Honolulu: University of Hawaiʻi Press, 2011.

Oi, Cynthia. "Shakin' Tradition." *Honolulu Star-Bulletin,* March 16, 2000.

"Portrait of Rosalie Lokalia Montgomery." Hawaii State Foundation on Culture and the Arts. State of Hawaii. Web. http://dags.hawaii.gov/sfca/app/gallery/displayimage.php?album=1&pid=39863.

Quill, Jenny. "Ancient Hula Hawaiian Style." *Honolulu,* September 7, 2010.

Seiden, Allan. *The Art of Hula.* Honolulu: Island Heritage Publishing, 2008.

Sen, Benton. *Men of Hula: Robert Cazimero and Halau Nā Kamalei.* Honolulu: Island Heritage Publishing, 2010.

Shaka, Angeline. "Hula." Dance Heritage Coalition, 2012. Web. http://www.danceheritage.org/treasures/hula_essay_shaka.pdf.

Shaka, Angeline. "Hula for the Future: Patrick Makuakāne and the Hula Mua 'Salva Mea.'" *Theatre Journal* 67, no. 3, October 2015.

Siler, Julia Flynn. "Aloha, Lady Gaga: A New Wave Of Hula Gains Sway on the Mainland—Hawaiians Say Some Dancers Have Gone Off the Island; Accused of a 'Lap Dance.'" *Wall Street Journal,* November 16, 2011.

Silva, Kalena. "The ʻŪniki of Maiki Aiu Lake's Papa Lehua." Study guide from *Biography Hawaʻii: Five Lives.* Hawaiʻi Public Television and the Center for Biographical Research of the University of Hawaiʻi–Mānoa. Web. http://www.hawaii.edu/biograph/pdf/maikiguide.pdf.

Silva, Wendell, and Alan Suemori, eds. *Nānā I Na Loea Hula: Look to the Hula Resources,* vol. 1. Honolulu: Kalihi-Palama Culture and Arts Society, 1984.

Simon, Liza. "A Tale of Two Kumu." *Hana Hou*, February/March 2011.

Stagner, Dr. Ishmael W. *Kumu Hula Roots and Branches*. Honolulu: Island Heritage Publishing, 2011.

Stillman, Amy Kuʻuleialoha. "'Aloha Aina: New Perspectives on 'Kaulana Na Pua.'" *Hawaiian Journal of History*, vol. 33, 1999.

Stillman, Amy Kuʻuleialoha. "Bibliography of Hula." In *The Hula*, edited by Jerry Hopkins. Honolulu: APA Productions, 1982.

Stillman, Amy Kuʻuleialoha. "Hula in Hawaii." In *International Encyclopedia of Dance*, edited by Selma Jeanne Cohen et al. New York: Oxford University Press, 1998.

Stillman, Amy Kuʻuleialoha. "Passed into the Present: Women in Hawaiian Entertainment." In *Asian/Pacific Islander American Women: A Historical Anthology*, edited by Shirley Hune and Gail M. Nomura. New York: New York University Press, 2003.

Stillman, Amy Kuʻuleialoha. *Sacred Hula: The Historical Hula ʻAlaʻapapa. Bishop Museum Bulletin in Anthropology* 8. Honolulu: Bishop Museum Press, 1998.

Tarleton, Catherine. "The Ties That Bind Us." *Mana: A Journal of Hawaiʻi*, March 28, 2016.

Tatar, Elizabeth. *Hula Pahu: Hawaiian Drum Dances, Vol. 2: The Pahu: Sounds of Power. Bishop Museum Bulletin in Anthropology* 3. Honolulu: Bishop Museum Press, 1993.

Tatar, Elizabeth. *Nineteenth-Century Hawaiian Chant*. Honolulu: Bernice Pauahi Bishop Museum, 1982.

Viotti, Vicki. "50 Years of Strict, but Gentle, Guidance in Hula." *Honolulu Advertiser*, April 5, 2002.

Wikipedia. "Iolani Luahine." Web. https://en.wikipedia.org/w/index.php?title=Iolani_Luahine&oldid=7179 49093.

Wolf, Sara. "Of Myths and Missionaries: 'The Natives Are Restless' Does Some Debunking." *Los Angeles Times*, April 5, 2004.

Wu, Nina. "Kumu Hula's Spirit 'Would Fill the Room and Beyond.'" *Honolulu Star-Advertiser*, September 29, 2015.

Wu, Nina. "Past to Present: Stories in Old Hawaiian-Language Newspapers Inspire a Hula Halau's New Stage Production." *Honolulu Star-Advertiser*, May 9, 2014.

Index

Photo Credits

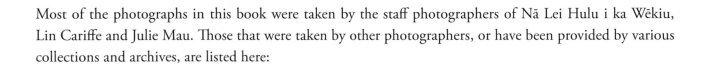

Most of the photographs in this book were taken by the staff photographers of Nā Lei Hulu i ka Wēkiu, Lin Cariffe and Julie Mau. Those that were taken by other photographers, or have been provided by various collections and archives, are listed here:

Page 47   **Sky and ocean:** Photo courtesy of Nā Lei Hulu i ka Wēkiu

Page 61   **Various pahu:** Photo courtesy of Kumu Hula Bradley Cooper

Page 63   **Kalākaua:** Courtesy of Hawai'i State Archives

Page 64   *Danse des hommes* **illustration:** Courtesy of Hawai'i State Archives

Page 73   **Patrick Makuakāne at 'Ōhikilolo Ranch, 1980s:** Photo by Wayne Iha

Page 78   **Aunti Maiki:** Photo courtesy of Lee Puake'ala Malakua Mann

Page 79   **'Ūniki Papa Laua'e 2003:** Photo by Wayne Iha

Page 80   **Aunti Mae:** Photo by Wayne Iha

Page 81   **The Sunday Mānoa:** Photo courtesy of Robert Cazimero

Page 82   **John Keola Lake:** Photo courtesy of Joshua 'Iwi Lake

Page 86   **Original dancers:** Photo by Patrick Makuakāne

Page 97   **Kumu Hula Francine Aarona, Mae Klein, Kalei Aarona-Lorenzo:** Photo by Wayne Iha

Page 112   **Alyce Ku'ualoha:** Photo courtesy of Patrick Makuakāne

Page 122   **Makuakāne family:** Photo courtesy of Patrick Makuakāne

Page 142   **Eleanor Prendergast:** Courtesy of Hawai'i State Archives

Page 144   **Aloha 'Āina Unity March, Waikīkī, 2015:** Photo by Shawn Kaho'olemana Naone

Page 144   **Mauna Kea:** Photo courtesy of Nā Lei Hulu i ka Wēkiu

Page 181   **Hula Show bus ad:** Photo by Patrick Makuakāne

Page 185   **Dancers with Roberta Flack:** Photo by Rob Edwards

Page 205   **Kini Wilson:** Courtesy of Hawai'i State Archives

Pages 224–225   **Ho'ike Nui:** Photo by Patrick Makuakāne

About the Author

photo by Elisa Pelayo

CONSTANCE HALE is a San Francisco–based journalist who has been writing about Hawaiian culture for more than twenty-five years. Her award-winning profiles and features on hula, slack-key guitar, the sovereignty movement, the Hawaiian language, Big Island cowboys, and Spam musubi have appeared in the *Atlantic, National Geographic Adventure, Afar, Smithsonian, Los Angeles Times, Miami Herald,* and *Honolulu.* She has written three books on language and literary style: *Wired Style, Sin and Syntax,* and *Vex, Hex, Smash, Smooch.* She has also written a book for children, *ʻIwalani's Tree.* It is set on Oʻahu's North Shore, where she was born and grew up. Hale started dancing the hula at seven, switching to ballet and jazz dance while in high school and college. She has studied hula with Patrick Makuakāne for twenty years.

Mālamalama ʻo Kapalakiko